Rookie Dad
Tackles the Toddler

SUSAN FOX

POCKET BOOKS
New York   London   Toronto   Sydney

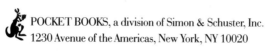 POCKET BOOKS, a division of Simon & Schuster, Inc.
1230 Avenue of the Americas, New York, NY 10020

Copyright © 2005 by Susan Fox

Photos courtesy of the author
Photography by Julie Chi, Dan DeLong, and Jane Lee

Library of Congress Cataloging-in-Publication Data

Fox, Susan.
 Rookie dad tackles the toddler / Susan Fox.
  p. cm.
 Sequel to: Rookie dad.
 ISBN: 1-4165-0323-4 (trade pbk.)
  1. Toddlers—Care. 2. Father and child. 3. Parenting—Handbooks,
manuals, etc. I. Title.
HQ774.5.F69 2005
649'.122—dc22   2005043101

First Pocket Books trade paperback edition June 2005

10 9 8 7 6 5 4 3 2 1

POCKET and colophon are registered trademarks of Simon & Schuster, Inc.

Manufactured in the United States of America

For information regarding special discounts for bulk purchases,
please contact Simon & Schuster Special Sales at 1-800-456-6798
or business@simonandschuster.com.

Dedicated to:
Dr. T. Berry Brazelton, who helped show me the way

If I Can Stop One Heart from Breaking

If I can stop one heart from breaking,
I shall not live in vain;
If I can ease one life the aching,
Or cool one pain,
Or help one fainting robin
Unto his nest again,
I shall not live in vain.

Emily Dickinson

Table of Contents

CONTENTS

Foreword

Your baby is not a blob anymore. That baby who seemed to want nothing but sleep, food, and a dry diaper has morphed into a nonstop motion machine who now melts your heart because he's just said, "I love you, Daddy." And just minutes before that, he tried to stuff a peanut butter and jelly sandwich into your DVD player.

You know the next few years are going to be long ones. Toddlers can drive the most sane person into a straitjacket; chaos follows them wherever they roam. Your briefcase, cell phone, and keys are not safe anymore. If you can get into the bathroom alone, you'll likely spend that time fishing your watch out of the toilet and noticing that your toddler has unspooled an entire roll of toilet paper.

Of course, that begs the question, what was the bathroom door doing open in the first place? That's the thing about toddlers. You're a team. Sometimes you're the coach, trying to lead your little son or daughter to victory. Sometimes you're the goalie, trying to see that they don't bury your wallet in a dog bowl of Alpo.

And if you're smart, you're going to enjoy every minute of it.

Time is short. Your child looks up to you and wants to be

with you more than anyone else right now. You may have been a nerd in school. Your girlfriend or wife may treat you with the sort of respect usually reserved for bumbling dads in sitcoms. Your dog may chew your new sneakers, and your boss is probably hoping to outsource your job to a teenager in India. But to your son or daughter, you are a hero. Don't waste or take their love for granted. Very quickly, they'll grow up and prefer watching a video or being with their friends. Make your time with them count; you'll never get it back.

So please—go to the park with your tot, go grocery shopping, take a ride in the car. It can be the simplest of tasks that you share with your son or daughter. When your kid looks back at life with Dad, his best memories won't be of expensive toys or of TV shows watched, but of time shared with you. That's why every day, you should make time in your day to play. Nothing is more important—not your job, not answering your email, not paying bills. Sure, those things are important—the electric company tends to appreciate a check every month. But your number one priority should be your child.

When you're eighty-five and looking back on the vast landscape that was your life, I guarantee you won't say to yourself, "I wish I'd worked more." The *last* thing you want to do is wish that you'd had a better relationship with your child. And that relationship doesn't begin when they're old enough to appreciate the nuances of a triple play, or when they're sixteen and need you to teach them to drive. It starts the day of birth and solidifies during the toddler years—when their personalities are forming. These are some of the most important years to show them that you care.

So make every day count. Tell and show your kids that you

love them. Give hugs, wrestle, shake hands, hit the playground, read stories, and take plenty of photos of that wonderful child you have.

Easier said than done, of course. In my work with parents at Microsoft, I see mothers and fathers who work long hours. Then during the time they have together, quality time is in short supply. But as demanding as your job or toddler is, we know who should always win out in the end. And if your child wins out, you'll win. Your toddler has lots of lessons to teach you—lessons about patience, unconditional love, and joy. And every minute with them is a vacation from the more challenging, frequently unsympathetic grown-up world.

So start vacationing. Now.

We never know how long each of us has.

CHAPTER 1

Brain Gym: Colors, Sizes, and Shapes

It's a well-known fact that intelligent dads usually have intelligent kids, which means that the next Einstein could be sitting in your living room watching *Teletubbies*. But when it comes to "smarts," genes aren't everything. Nurture is just as important as nature, and you can give even the brightest toddler a boost in the learning department by providing brain exercise in the form of new experiences.

Right now, your child's brain is literally under construction. Over the next two years, trillions of connections will form between her brain cells, and those connections will help determine everything, from how well she'll speak a foreign language to how good she'll be at trigonometry, history, or quantum physics. Every interesting new experience you offer her—petting a goat, smelling a flower, reading a new book—will build new connections, and those connections translate into increased brainpower.

Show her how bathtub toys float and how rocks dropped into a puddle sink. Buy her a set of toy tools, and show her how they work. Have her put her hands on her chest, to feel her own heartbeat and breathing, and then let her do the same to you. Let her watch and help (or at least think she's helping!) as you fold the laundry, vacuum the car, cook a meal, hammer a nail, or play a musical instrument. Take bus rides together to parks, stores, and restaurants. These real-life lessons will stick with your child much longer than anything she'd learn from a worksheet.

A TODDLER "LESSON PLAN"

Though most parents want to start with academic skills, such as counting and reading, you're better off teaching these skills at the preschool or elementary school stage, when your child is ready to master them. Instead work on basic thinking skills, including:

- *Problem solving.* Stacking toys, big keys and locks, nesting toys, shape sorters, simple puzzles, oversized nuts and bolts, and blocks will stimulate your toddler's gray matter. Have him sort toys, nuts, books, and balls by size. And give him some everyday challenges. For instance, say, "Your toys won't fit in your toy box. What should we do?" Ask him, "Where does the water in the hose come from?" and turn the water on and off at the spigot so that he begins to learn cause and effect.

- *Discrimination.* Work on the concepts of *same* and *different.* For instance, show her three spoons and one cup, and say, "What's different?" "What's the same?"

• *Memory.* Let your toddler watch while you hide plastic animals, spoons, or small toys under a cloth, and then ask, "Where did Daddy put it?" Also, show her photos of recent events—a holiday, family gathering, or birthday party—and ask her about the people in the photos.

• *Imaginative play.* Foster your child's creativity by playing imagination games. For instance, pretend that you're both cars and race around the yard, or pretend that you're animals in the zoo. Play games where she feeds her dolly or Dad. Play barber or beauty shop, or grocery store, or stage a puppet show.

Also, buy her a play doctor's kit, a toy vacuum cleaner, a telephone, a toy lawn mower, pretend food, tools, or other toys that will let her play at being a grown-up. Pass on some of your old clothes, too; your toddler will love dressing up in your old hats, socks, and shoes, or even lugging around an old briefcase.

SHOW AND TELL HELPS

When you're explaining new concepts to your toddler, repetition is crucial, and it may take five, ten, or even more tries for your toddler to learn a new piece of information. Also, hands-on learning is likely to stick in her head far better than lectures. You can talk about "bigger" and "smaller" all day long, but you're better off grabbing a glob of Play-Doh, showing her how to make tiny, medium-sized, and huge clay snakes, and then letting her try it herself.

Similarly, you can illustrate the concept of *through* very

simply by sticking a straw through a cookie or a ball of Play-Doh. If you're teaching her words like *under, on,* and *through,* create an obstacle course that involves crawling under tables, climbing over pillows, and going through tunnels. Use blocks to illustrate *tall* and *short,* or glasses of water to show the difference between *cool* and *warm.*

QUESTIONS . . . AND MORE QUESTIONS . . .

Talking to your toddler is important too, especially when it comes to answering her questions. Her endless questions may drive you crazy at times, but she needs to learn a million facts about her universe, and you're the person she trusts the most to have straight answers. The constant questioning of toddlers starts early, with a one-year-old's "What's that?" and advances to a two- to three-year-old's "Why is the sun warm?" and similar toughies.

Try to answer every question your toddler dreams up, using simple language she can understand. (Of course, you don't need to answer *every* question fully. One of my favorite overheard conversations in a grocery store went like this: "Daddy, what's this?" "It's a box of Tampax." "What's it for?" "It's for ladies." "What do they do with it?" "They stick it in the bathroom cabinet. Now"—note of desperation in Dad's voice—"let's go pick out some cookies!")

NO TIME?

If you're one of those lucky dads who's home every night and every weekend, it won't be hard to find opportunities to teach your child about her world. But if you're so swamped with overtime work or other obligations that you don't have time to make Play-Doh snakes, build obstacle courses, or take your child to the zoo, you can still give your toddler's brain cells a workout even if you can only spare ten or fifteen minutes at bedtime. How? *Just by picking up a book.*

Reading is one of the most important learning activities you can share with your child, because children who are read to have larger vocabularies and do better in school than other children. So if your work schedule allows, start a bedtime-story reading ritual with your toddler. In addition to teaching her new words and exposing her to new worlds, a cuddle with Dad and a bedtime-story session at the same time each night will relax her and help her fall asleep—which means that you might get a chance to read a little of your *own* book!

When you read to your toddler, let her be involved in the story you're telling. Ask, "What did the lion say?" or say, "Show me the dog." Ask her to turn the pages for you; she'll enjoy participating. To improve her memory skills, ask her if she remembers what happened in earlier parts of the story. And relate the stories to her own life: If you're reading about ice cream, go open the freezer and look at the ice cream you have. If possible, insert her name into the story as you're reading.

WHEN SITTING STILL TO HEAR A STORY IS A PROBLEM

If you have a squirmy toddler who has trouble sitting still for long, give her a small toy to hold. Pick one that relates to the book; for instance, if you're reading about toy cars, have her hold a car. Encourage her to hold her toy car up to the picture of the car in the book, so she can develop the concept that pictures represent real objects. Kids often enjoy reading a story while rocking in a rocking chair.

NOT THAT BOOK AGAIN . . .

Your brain may recoil at the idea of reading *The Very Hungry Caterpillar* for the hundred-and-sixty-seventh time, but a familiar book is as great a joy to your toddler as that well-worn tape of *Terminator II* is to you. If your toddler wants to read her favorite books over and over and over again, let it happen. As you read the same stories over and over, your child will naturally begin making the connection between the story you're telling and the words she sees on the page.

MAKE IT FUN, NOT HARD WORK

It is fun to find and trace letters with fingers and to go on a letter hunt. Your child will soon be able to spot the first letter of her name and *D* for *Dad* every time it turns up. Bring the pages of books to life for your child with funny voices, entertaining sound effects, and insightful Dad-type commentary, and make reading time a fun time with lots of cuddling and praise. Reading with Dad *is* fun!

The more you play with your toddler today, the better off she'll be when she sets foot in the classroom. And ask yourself this: When you look back on your own life, do you say, "Gee, I wish I'd spent more time with flash cards?"

Give your toddler a nature lesson by letting her help you

plant a garden. Give her a cooking lesson by showing her how to make instant pudding. Give her a physics lesson in the bathroom; flush the toilet and let her watch the water swirl down. Introduce her to the ants and earthworms in your backyard, and water the yard together so she can learn how water comes out of the hose.

"Daddy Delivers"

Eighteen months to three years

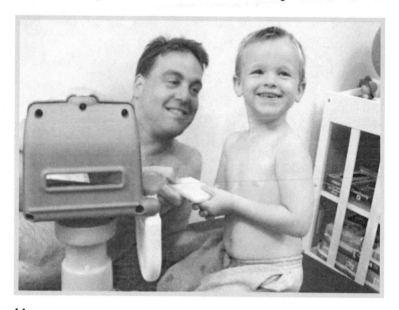

Kids love getting mail, even a scrap of paper. For a younger toddler, write your child a short note, draw a picture, a doodle, even a stick figure of Dad, or cut out a picture of an animal from a magazine.

An older child can "dictate" a letter to you, other family members, or even your family pet. Put the picture or letter into an envelope your child can open. Write your child's name on the outside, and add a picture of a stamp. Make a mailbox, and then practice "delivering" the mail.

Game tip: *You can make a mailbox out of a cardboard shoe box, or buy a small mailbox at the hardware store.*

"Laundry Basket Rebound"

One to four years

Give Mom a hand and earn some bonus points. It's a great way to learn new words and practice grasping and releasing objects. (Handy for that first trout-fishing trip.) Sorting laundry teaches your child how to match and put things in order.

- Find all the socks, washrags, and towels, and practice tossing different items of laundry into a basket.
- Have your child help you sort laundry by color—white socks and dark socks. Sort laundry by big and little socks, towels, etc.

Game tip: *Kids love playing peekaboo in the basket. Throw a shirt or towel over your toddler's head and say, "Where's (child's name)?" Act surprised when the towel or shirt falls off.*

"Best Foot Forward"

One to two years

Help kids learn *mine* and *yours* (everything is *mine* to a toddler). There's a top-notch toy waiting in the closet: all toddlers are fascinated by shoes. Filling Dad's shoes is a tall order, but lots of fun!

- Take a couple of pairs of Dad's shoes and a pair of your child's shoes.
- Let your toddler try putting his shoes into yours.
- Kids who can walk think it's very cool to stand in Dad's shoes.
- Explore the contrast of big and little shoes, *in,* and *out.*

Game tip: *The laces of shoes can be a choking hazard, so consider removing them before playing.*

"Where's the Ball?"

One to three years

Share the fun and excitement of opening a gift every day. Cardboard boxes make great hiding places. Sharpen your child's memory and teach patience at the same time!

- Let your toddler watch you wrap a toy and put it in a cardboard box.
- Ask your child to find the toy he watched you wrap and place in the box.
- Find two toys that will fit in your hands. Open your hands so your toddler can see what's in them and say, "Where's the *(one toy)?*" or "Where's the *(other toy)?*" Once he masters this step, close your hands and say, "Where's the *(one toy)?*" or "Where's the *(other toy)?*"

Game tip: *You can also play these games by hiding objects in your pockets. Ask your child to find the toy in your pocket and let him reach in and grab it.*

"The Toddler Free Throw"

One to three years

Kids love helping Dad unload the family's groceries.

• Hand your toddler safe items to carry.
• With kids over two, you can get some early T-ball practice. Have your child catch soft items like a package of napkins, or a loaf of bread.
• You can also play I Spy while unpacking groceries. For example, "I spy something hard, soft, crackly. Can you find it, too?"

Game tip: *Have Dad carry cleaning supplies, eggs, and groceries in glass containers.*

"Bowling for Brainpower"

Two to three years

Who knew that bowling could build fine motor skills and teach kids how to follow directions?

• Place plastic or soft bowling pins on the floor or a low table.
• Have your child roll a soft ball at the pins.
• Count how many pins have been knocked over.

Game tip: *Practice rolling the ball back and forth to each other to show your child how to keep the ball on the floor.*

"Pop-Up Play"

One to two years

Does your child cry when you leave? Here's a great toy that shows your child that Dad will always come back. A guaranteed winner, this toy helps your child get more comfortable with separation. It also builds memory skills and the understanding that things exist when you can't see them.

This is a great game that helps your child practice learning to wait and persistence.

• Start with a jack-in-the-box in open position.
• Help your child push the toy down into the box.
• Ask your child, "Where did the toy go?"
• "Let's find it by pushing the roller/crank."
• Help your child as needed until the toy pops up.
• "You did it! Let's do it again."

Game tip: Purchase an easy-to-open jack-in-the-box that uses a roller, not a tiny crank.

"Hole in One"

One year to eighteen months

Here's a favorite brainteaser that builds memory and listening skills, as well as fine motor coordination.

• Use a cardboard tube, as well as some small toys or finger food such as Cheerios, Goldfish crackers, or a ball.
• Hand your child the object and ask him to put it in the tube.
• Ask, "Where did it go?"

Game tip: Check small toys to be sure they are not a choking hazard.

"Eye on the Ball"

One to three years

Want to build your kid's brainpower? Playing this game will help him recognize differences in size and shape—a handy skill when he learns to read, too.

- You'll need two balls, one small and one large.
- Ask your child, "Where's the big ball?"
- Use a big loud voice when saying "big."
- Ask your child, "Where's the little ball?"
- Use a softer, quieter voice when saying "small."
- Get additional practice exploring hard and soft, cold and hot, or wet and dry washcloths.

Game tip: *Choose items that are the same color to help your child identify differences in size or shape.*

TIPS FOR WINNING

Be understanding if your toddler loses interest and wanders off when you're only partway through an interesting explanation of how birds fly, or why snow melts. She's not being rude; she's simply not capable of paying attention for more than a few minutes at a stretch. When she's older, she'll ignore you on purpose; right now, however, it's unintentional.

See what interests your child intellectually, and follow her lead. For instance, if birds fascinate her, buy a bird feeder and help her sprinkle birdseed in it every day. If she likes to make music, pick up a triangle, some maracas, or a harmonica. A budding mechanic? Buy her a toy workbench and tools.

Let your child know his questions are important. If you're rushing off to work and don't have time to answer one of those complicated queries ("Daddy, why don't fish drown?"), promise that you'll get back to him later, rather than merely saying, "I'm too busy for that now." (And don't forget to get back to him!)

Educational supply stores aren't just for teachers. These stores are wonderful sources of toddler treasures, including mind-stretching games, books, and toys. They're also great places to take a toddler, because almost everything in them is unbreakable.

Introduce your toddler to the library or bookstore, and let him choose his own books. (Steer him toward virtually indestructible cardboard books.) At home, put his selections on a special bookshelf, and let him pick one each night at story time.

Resist the urge to correct your child each time he mispronounces a word slightly or makes a minor grammatical error. He'll pick up correct grammar and pronunciation eventually, simply by listening to grown-ups talking.

THE SAFETY ZONE

Small toys intended for older children (such as Lego and Playmobil sets) are a choking hazard. Keep them well out of your toddler's reach. Set aside gifts that aren't yet safe for later. Whistles aren't good toys for toddlers. Small parts can be broken from the whistle and inhaled.

The great outdoors is full of learning opportunities, but make sure your toddler is safe when he's out in your front or back yard. Teach him to stay away from the driveway, and keep him away from garage doors, because even those with safety mechanisms can sometimes fail and trap a child underneath. And always stay with him, even if he's just going outside for a minute or two.

Teach your toddler to ask permission, both from you and from a pet's owner, before he or she approaches or touches any dog or cat. It's good manners, and it can prevent a serious bite or scratch.

Kids under two stick tiny toys and objects, such as wads of paper or gum, into their noses and ears. Toddlers may also try to swallow pennies. Keep an eagle eye when small objects are in close range, especially when out and about.

Throw away antifreeze and drain cleaner, or put them in a locked cabinet. Put a lock on your medicine cabinet. Keep vitamins, mouthwash, and all medicines up high. Kids think of vitamins as candy; caustic liquids can look like juice.

SPECIAL PLAYS

Play classical music, show tunes, or jazz at dinnertime. It'll put everyone in a mellow mood and help your toddler develop an ear for good music.

Read the backs of cereal boxes together at the breakfast table. Your toddler won't recognize the words yet, but he'll enjoy looking at the bright colors while you do the reading.

Get "down and dirty" with your toddler every once in a while. (Dads are usually better at this than moms are.) Play in the leaves, give your child a mini-lesson in geography by building mud rivers and mountains together, or teach him about different shapes by making sand castles, using a variety of cups, bowls, square food containers, toilet paper tubes, and pails to mold your masterpieces.

While your toddler's too young to learn addition or subtraction, you can incorporate counting into his games. Count,

"One, two, three!" as he jumps, or count his blocks as he stacks them up. As he hears you count out loud, he'll begin to learn the names of numbers.

Make personalized books for your child, using photos and stories about his pets, family members, trips, special events, or even everyday activities. Or, if you're into computers, create "virtual" books and post them on your toddler's very own website.

Help your child learn to categorize objects by sorting them—for instance, foods, books, cars, and animals.

Put cardboard books in the car. They may get chewed on, but your toddler will learn to love reading in the car on car trips later. Books that have flaps with pictures underneath build memory.

Name vehicles—cars, trucks, cement mixers, bulldozers—while traveling around town.

If you have a workshop, let your child help sort scrap wood, large nuts, and bolts.

CALL FOR THE REFEREE

Your kid is number one. Of course your daughter is the smartest kid in play group. Your son can recite *Cat in the Hat* from memory, and anyone can see he's headed for Harvard. It's just that the other parents won't admit these obvious truths. You know that comparing your kid with the others roving the sandbox can create problems. Talking to your partner about those other parents and kids will help you keep your perspective.

When you come home, the house always seems to be a disaster area, with toys everywhere. It is amazing how much mess a toddler can make. Partners may disagree about how many toys a child actually needs to have and how much money should be spent for toys, but there is no way you are going to have a completely neat house when you have a toddler unless you keep her in her room 24/7. Ease up, pitch in, and help with the pickup.

How important is it to enroll your toddler in music, art, gymnastics, and preschool classes? You wonder if you should take your toddler to a toddler music class that's starting on Saturdays nearby. He can't sit still very long, but lots of the other kids in the neighborhood are going. Your partner may think it's too expensive, but you don't want your child left out. A music class that encourages movement in addition to listening might be just the ticket for a musical adventure and help your little wiggler channel some of that energy, too. However, you might want your Saturdays free for downtime. Couples often have different views about the need for educational classes for toddlers. Take a look at the budget, as well as the calendar, together.

ADVICE FROM THE COACH

My kid loves Baby Einstein *videos and* Sesame Street *on television. How much TV/video is okay? And does it hurt their brain development and learning?*

Watching an hour or two a day of TV or videos doesn't do any harm to your child's brain development or learning potential. Sitting down in front of educational videos that feature animals, trains, music, and the like builds vocabulary and independence. It also helps both parents and kids unwind. Research supports the notion that children who achieve academic success can benefit from limited amounts of educational TV or videos. Young children do not benefit from watching violent television, including the news, wrestling, and most cartoons.

Our toddler always wants me to play with him. When will he learn to play on his own? How can I help make that happen?

Sit next to your child and encourage him to play independently. For example, provide commentary while your child is building with blocks. Say, "I like how you are building that tower all by yourself." Gradually increase the physical distance between you and your child, and continue to provide support and praise as he plays independently. Kids begin to play on their own sometime between eighteen months and two and a half years old.

Our three-year-old likes to listen to books on tape. Can I play these for her at bedtime?

Story tapes have their place, but they're no substitute for a warm, cuddly, interactive dad. A tape won't stop to explain a word your toddler doesn't know, or read the best parts over again, or laugh along at the funny parts. It's okay to supplement story reading with tapes, but your toddler will get far more enjoyment and mental stimulation when you perform "live." Books on tape can help on long car rides, though, if you can stand the story line.

My two-year-old loves to move my computer mouse and play with my keyboard. Is he ready for his own software?
Yes! Good software programs for toddlers include *Jump Start Baby, Jump Start Toddler, Reader Rabbit Toddler,* and *Millie & Bailey Preschool.* At first, let your toddler simply enjoy manipulating the mouse, looking at the bright colors, and listening to the music. If he's ready to start recognizing colors, letters, and numbers, fine; if not, don't push him.

Your toddler will also enjoy sitting on your lap while you play grown-up computer games—but stick to innocuous games such as *The Sims* or *Railroad Tycoon,* and avoid blood-and-guts games like *Quake* (unless you want to pay for years of therapy later). Let him move the mouse occasionally, and talk about what's happening on the screen. ("Look—Daddy just connected Philadelphia and Pittsburgh by rail, and his stock split twice!") He won't understand the game, but he'll pick up new words and learn that computers are entertaining.

Some toddlers can manipulate a regular mouse easily, while others have difficulty. If yours is one of the latter, try a Microsoft EasyBall, which has an oversized trackball and a big button. Kid-sized keyboards are also available, but they're expensive and aren't really necessary.

My child doesn't like to be read to. He has trouble sitting still and wants to get up and go after a few minutes of being read to, or he keeps turning the pages.
Start with books with few words to a page and lots of pictures. Talk about the pictures and let your child turn the page and

then talk about the next pictures. Have your toddler hold a toy that relates to the story—a car or an animal are two that work. Keep your reading sessions short—just a few minutes—and lengthen them as your toddler's attention span grows. Be sure to have story time at a time of day when your toddler has eaten and has had some big-muscle exercise. Bedtime is the perfect time for most youngsters.

CHAPTER 2

Kid Talk: Speech, Language, and Listening

Communication might seem like an arena mostly meant for moms. Like *Home Improvement*'s Tim "The Tool Man" Taylor, you may be content to make your thoughts and wishes known with the clipped talk and gestures of an NFL referee. But now that you're a dad of a toddler, you're discovering that communication is the key to stress reduction—both yours and your toddler's.

You've already figured out that most one- to three-year-olds have a very limited understanding of language, and even less ability to talk. Their specialties are whining, screaming, grunting, and gesturing. Their conversations are limited to words of one or two syllables at best. But what might be incomprehensible to a stranger is actually a code that you, as a dad, have been learning to decipher.

You've had a head start, since in his first year you already learned many of the basics—rubbing his eyes when he's sleepy, whimpering when he's hungry, and the grunt that's your early warning that he's going to have a really stinky diaper soon. But now he's a toddler, and the range of thoughts and needs he is communicating has increased dramatically. Unfortunately, his ability to use words has not kept pace. This, in a nutshell, is the source of the frustration that is a major factor in legendary toddler tantrums and unpleasant behavior of all sorts.

GESTURES AND SOUND EFFECTS— WHO NEEDS WORDS?

Even before your toddler is using words and sentences regularly, he can begin communicating with sound effects and gestures. Actually, a toddler's grunt-and-point is not unlike the language of manly grunts (though of course there are many refinements in tone and innuendo that you have mastered over the years). You, as Dad, may well have a head start on Mom in this early communication.

When your toddler starts screeching and looks poised to hurl a partially eaten plate of noodles, peas, and apple slices off his tray, you move quickly to remove the potential projectiles. Then you look him in the eye and say, "You're all done. You want down. All done. Down." You can accompany the words with hand gestures of pushing the dish away and pointing down. He will learn that there is another, more positive way to be excused from the table than the flying-food routine. And after you repeat this lesson a number of times, one day he will ask either verbally ("All done") or by gesture (pushing the plate away and pointing down) to be excused from the table. You will praise his efforts, do the Daddy end-dance of victory, and let him down.

SAY WHAT?

Grunts, screams, and whines are signals of frustration—you can find the clues in your child's behavior that tell you what's going on. Your little champ is not trying to embarrass you with his Cro-Magnon communication skills, he's just trying to make himself understood in the only way he can. This method of communication is the beginning of speech.

BABY'S FIRST WORDS

Hearing your toddler say "Dada" for the first time will bring you a rush unmatched by an Olympic gold medal. Some of the most common first words your toddler will learn are likely to be the names of the people and objects most important to him—*mamma, daddy, binky, babba.* Have you ever stopped to think about how many times a baby hears the word *Hi?* Or *no-no?* No wonder they often get fixated on those words, repeating them over and over. *Hi* and *Bye-bye* are typically some of the first words your baby learns, and with reason. Encourage your toddler to greet people with "Hi" and "Bye-bye."

Even though he may not be able to say more than four or five words yet, your toddler is filing away words and their meanings at an amazing rate. Between the ages of one and two, your toddler can understand about three thousand words. By the time he's three, the number of words he understands will rocket to an amazing ten thousand.

VOLUME CONTROL

Every parent has probably marveled at the decibels these little people can produce. Even happy shrieks and screeches can approach the volume of a crowd of 20,000 rowdy fans at a football game. An important contribution you can make in the toddler years is to teach the distinction between indoor and outdoor voices. While your lung capacity is larger than his, and you could, in theory, out-yell your child, it's not an effective approach.

Instead, show him that using his biggest voice is fine outside during playtime, but drop your own volume when you tell him, "When we're inside, we use quiet voices."

PENALTIES AND FOULS

One of the most powerful uses for language is expressing feelings. This may sound like the premise of every *Oprah* episode, but your interactions with your toddler will soon convince you. Your child needs the ability to distinguish between emotions like sad, mad, scared, and frustrated.

When you observe him feeling frustrated say, "You are frustrated. When you feel that way, you can ask for help. You are frustrated because you can't reach your ball. Ask me to help." You can also help him label his feelings by explaining your own. For example, if you get separated at the football game, you can explain, "I was looking for you for a long time and I couldn't find you. I don't want you to get lost, I need you with me."

Offer commentary. Think of yourself as a sportscaster offering a play-by-play on your child's game of life. When a play date threatens to erupt into punches and kicks, step in, separate the combatants, and say, "Noah, you want the truck that Olivia is playing with. When you took the truck, Olivia felt mad. Olivia, you are mad. When you're mad, use words. You cannot hit."

SPEECH 101

You are bound to get some signals crossed, misread some cues, and feel like you need a translator who is fluent in toddler screams. Everyday activities are the best opportunities for teaching language. Rather than simply handing your toddler a snack in silence while you're absorbed in the sports page, take five minutes to do a little language coaching. Make eye contact and ask, "Want a cracker?" Then wait for his response. At first you might need to gently use your hand to nod his head up and down, at the same time modeling what a yes nod looks like and saying "Yes, I want a cracker." Then ask, "Where are those crackers? Do you know where we keep crackers?" and allow him to point them out. "Here is the cracker box—in the cupboard. Let's each have a cracker." Not only have you just used the word *cracker* about ten times but you've also introduced other words and concepts in a natural context. You can introduce decision making by adding an alternative. Try asking, "Or do you want milk instead?" Again, wait for his response: pointing, looking at his choice, or an effort at saying *milk*. Even a simple trip to the Home Depot, a walk around the block, or washing the car in the driveway can be the occasion for a Toddler Speech 101 class. Your baby will absorb your commentary on the action from you, one of his favorite people in the whole world.

YES, NO, MAYBE SO

Toddlers love to shake their head for *no,* and *no* is possibly their favorite word. You can both pander to their taste for negativity and teach listening discrimination skills by playing simple, repetitive games. When putting on his socks, playfully put the sock on his nose, hands, ears, chin, asking, "Do socks go on your nose?" He will think you are funnier than David Letterman, practice his "No!" and incidentally learn to name some body parts. How's that for multitasking while getting socks on?

Your toddler's ability to give *yes* and *no* responses to questions can be a major communication breakthrough, but for the lessons to work, you have to let *no* be a viable option. So reserve *yes* or *no* questions for times when your child really does have a choice. It's not fair to ask, "Do you want to get into your car seat?" and then insist that he must get into his car seat even when your toddler clearly answers "No." It's fairer to your toddler and less confusing all around to make a clear statement: "It's time to get into your car seat." "You need a bath—let's get one now." "It's time for bed in two minutes." "This medicine will help you to feel better. After you take your medicine we can read a story."

READING AND SUCCEEDING

Reading with your child is the single most important way to build strong language skills. Reading sessions of only five minutes will give your child abilities that will last a lifetime.

At this age, board books are your best bet. They're virtually indestructible and tend to be short and sweet—perfect for the toddler attention span. If your toddler has a hard time sitting still, consider giving him a toy or finger puppet to help illustrate the story. Also, teach him how to turn pages. The sense of control will be heady to your little one, and you might even get a few pages read!

• *Vocabulary.* By the time she's two, your toddler will be learning as many as ten new words a day. Expand her vocabulary by reading her lots of books about her world—both the things she sees every day and the things she might not see herself (for instance, zoo animals, snow, the ocean, or the forest). Also, play the Name Game. Say all but the last word of a sentence, and let your toddler fill in the name of the object that should follow. For instance, "We're going to drive in the _____." If she needs help, cue her with the first letter of the word.

• *Listening skills and attention span.* These are key skills that your toddler will need to succeed in every school subject. Reading is an excellent way to improve listening and attention skills. So are songs that require your toddler to focus and pay attention, like "Old MacDonald."

- *Spatial relationships.* Help your child learn *up/down*, *under/over*, etc., by providing her with plenty of blocks, Legos, and other building tools. When you're stacking blocks or Legos together, ask questions such as, "What block do you want to put on top?" and "Can you put a block beside this block?" Put a doll on your leg, under your arm, on your head, or in your shirt pocket, and say, "Where's the dolly?" When she laughs and points, say, "Yes, the dolly is on my head."

- *Identifying and matching sights and sounds.* Ask your child to identify the sounds she hears around the house—for instance, the dog barking, the cat meowing, the dishwasher, or the telephone. To foster her visual skills, provide her with lots of picture books and colorful toys. Ask her to pick out different animals in a farm book and to tell what noises each animal makes. When you look at family photo albums, ask her to pick out favorite relatives, friends, or pets in the pictures.

- *Following directions.* To succeed at school, your child will need to carry out instructions. Give her opportunities to practice by giving her two-stage directions like "Take off your shoes and put your socks inside."

- *Sequencing.* Line up toys in a row: monkey first, then bear, last dog, to demonstrate the concepts of *first*, *next*, and *last*.

Ask questions while reading. If you're reading about dogs, ask, "Where's the dog?" Point to the dog if your toddler isn't quite ready to identify it yet, and he'll soon be showing off by pointing out dogs everywhere. You can also introduce more words through description. Try saying, "Look at the big dog. See, this little dog is the baby, and here is the big Daddy dog. Do you see this dog has spots?"

You can also use books as a springboard for a game of What's That? With a young toddler, you could start by looking at the pages of the childhood classic *Goodnight Moon*. Ask her, "Where's the moon?" Have her point to the moon on each page. As her language skills grow, point to objects and ask, "What's that?" She'll soon be identifying other objects: the red balloon, the little mouse, the toy house, the bowl full of mush, and the little old lady whispering "hush."

Cardboard books featuring a single photo on each page are available on a variety of topics, from farm animals to construction equipment. Some great books to read to your child are *Thomas the Tank Engine*, *Brown Bear*, and *The Very Hungry Caterpillar*, as are Margaret Wise Brown's *Goodnight Moon* and *Runaway Bunny*. Another to look for is Donald Carew's *Freight Train*. Don't be surprised to have your child beg for them over and over!

LOOK FOR BOOKS THAT ENCOURAGE ALL THE SENSES

You can also consider using books that have activities such as flaps to lift or tabs to pull. Some books have holes to poke fingers into or textures to touch that may captivate the reluctant reader. Others play songs, make animal noises, or provide sound effects to accompany the text. Some parents, however, find that these books can provoke temporary insanity, especially on long car rides or in combination with other loud toys. You can bring down the volume by taping over the sound box, but a more effective ploy is to remove fresh batteries and replace them with some that are nearing the end of their useful lives.

Be prepared to read your toddler's favorite book many times over, like a baseball game with endless innings. Once he has learned a story, he will probably catch you if you try to turn two pages at once, and he might object loudly if you skip lines. Don't expect him to appreciate any last-minute substitutions, either. His single-minded devotion to *Sheep in a Jeep* may exasperate you, but one day, you'll overhear him "reading" to himself, complete with the sound effects and commentary.

SPEECH COACH, NOT CRITIC

Most toddlers mispronounce words and develop their own unique renditions of words. The general rule of thumb that child development specialists offer is that by the age of three, most children can be understood by a non-family member most of the time. There is a broad spectrum of normal language development among toddlers, with girls typically being more advanced at an earlier age. If you are concerned that your child is not trying to communicate, or does not appear to understand you much of the time, it may be helpful to have him assessed by a professional.

"Calling All Dads"

One to three years

Show your child the ropes when it comes to meeting and greeting people. Playing "phone" with your toddler will also encourage early talking and good manners. The grandparents will be so pleased!

- This game requires two toy telephones.
- Give one to your child and hold one yourself.
- Pretend to call your child, and hold a conversation with him.
- Give him time to respond. He'll quickly pick up the idea.

Game tip: *Repeat whatever your child says—this is a great way to connect and keep up to date.*

"Power Moves"

One to three years

Kids imitate gestures before they learn words. Using gestures promotes imitation, an important step on the way to learning to talk. This is why you need to be careful which gestures you use in front of your child! Here are some that are kid-friendly.

- Demonstrate the hand movements to songs like "Itsy Bitsy Spider," "Open, Shut Them," or "Pat a Cake."
- Slowly demonstrate the movement. Encourage your child to copy you. Break it down into steps, follow your child.

Game tip: *Get in front of your child, or do this in front of a mirror.*

"Winning by a Nose"

One to three years

Your child is growing up, and so is her awareness of her body. She can learn to name body parts.

- Say, "This is your nose, this is Daddy's nose."
- Then ask, "Where's your nose?"
- Then ask your child, "Where's Daddy's nose?"
- Finally, ask your child to find her nose in a mirror.
- Help your child discover other parts of the body, such as tummy, head, toes, hair, and mouth.

Game tip: *Once you have a handle on eyes, ears, nose, hair, and head, try this game using a stuffed animal.*

"Pop Bubbles with Pop"

One to three years

This very fun activity will teach your child how to follow directions, language skills, and hand-eye coordination. It will also decrease drooling!

- Encourage your child to make the "O" sound.
- Blow bubbles and say, "What's that?"
- Emphasize "bbbbb-bubble," "buh" for bubbles.
- Practice popping bubbles together.

Game tip: *Kids over eighteen months like to help Dad blow bubbles, so buy bubbles in spill-proof containers. Kids over two may enjoy counting bubbles.*

"Off to the Races"

One to three years

Concepts like *stop* and *go* are important for toddlers to learn, to keep them from dashing across the park or into the street. This game is a fun variation on the old Red Light Green Light game you may have played as a child.

• Line up cars at the top of a slide.
• Say, "Ready, set, go!"
• Release the cars, and verbally note when each car stops.
• Kids over two can identify colors of the cars. Ask your child, "Which car finished first in the race?"

Game tip: *Soft rubber cars are fun and safer.*

"Reading the Stats"

One to three years

Need a good use for all the stuffed animals that seem to have multiplied in your home? Use them during story time with your toddler. This activity will help your child learn language, lengthen her attention span, and give her a head start on building her vocabulary.

- Take, for instance, a book about a crocodile and a stuffed crocodile (or other book-animal pairs).
- Encourage your child to turn the pages as you go.
- Bring the words to life as you read: growl like you're a crocodile, snap your fingers, or chomp your teeth.
- Let the toy crocodile bite your fingers and your child's hands.
- Let your child imitate your actions.

Game tip: *Substitute your child's name for a name in the book.*

"Leap Frog"

One to three years

Have your toddler follow Dad's lead and explore the concepts of *over* and *under.*

• Have your child lie down on the floor.
• Jump over your child.
• Hold your child as you leap over a stuffed frog.
• Hold the frog and have it leap over your child.
• Have your child hold the frog and make it leap over Dad.
• Play catch with the frog together.

Game tip: You can use a variety of animals and practice the sounds animals make while jumping over the animals.

"Jammin' with Dad"

One to three years

Get together some kid-sized instruments and have a jam session! Opportunities to count are everywhere in music. This is a great low-key way to learn some numbers.

- Play music fast and slow, quietly and loudly.
- Count "one, two, three, four" and get your kid to copy the pattern.

Game tip: *Musical toys without batteries are easier on your ears.*

"Cheers for the Mascot"

One year to thirty months

This activity helps your child learn to imitate sounds, which will help him learn to talk. It's always fun to pretend to be an animal and make growly sounds.

- Kids learn to make sounds before they learn to talk, and they love to copy animal noises.
- Encourage your child to imitate different animal sounds. For example, "What does a dog say?" "Woof."
- Encourage any sound that comes out, and repeat the sound.

Game tip: *Ever wonder what to do with all those stuffed animals? Use them to make sounds together.*

TIPS FOR WINNING

Read slowly and let your child turn the pages. As you near the last page of the book, mention that the book is almost done, helping her anticipate the end of the story.

Reps take on a new meaning to dads of toddlers. You're no longer pumping iron at the gym—you're reading the same book over and over, one hundred plus times, until your two-year-old has memorized every word and nuance in her favorite book. Predictability is important to toddlers. They like the fact that they know what's coming next in their favorite book.

Toddlers learn by imitation. They are watching and copying every facial cue, so read with plenty of expression—smiles, surprised looks, frowns, or scared expressions relating to the text. Use verbal expressions, too, like "Oohhh," "Uh-oh," and "Ummm" as part of your customized rendition of the text and pictures.

Provide sound effects. Your ability to replicate the purr of a finely tuned high-performance engine can finally be put to good use. Likewise, you can provide the *beep-beep* for a horn, the *whoo-whoo* of a train whistle, or the *bzzzz* of a saw. Your toddler will delight in every quack, woof, baaaa, neigh, oink, and meow. Throw in some lip smacks and tongue clicks for good measure.

Give your toddler the chance to request what he wants. Anticipating his every need and leaping to provide things before he asks will only foster the rock-star attitude you're trying to avoid. Remember, your goal is to create an independent, capable kid who can ask for what he wants, whether with words or gestures.

SAFETY ZONE

Loud noises can damage your toddler's hearing. Resist the urge to drown out your child's noise with louder noise of your own. If you let your child use headphones with his tape player or other electronic equipment, check the volume level and be sure that he can't turn it up and blast his eardrums.

Loud toys can be toned down with a piece of thick tape placed securely over the speaker. You may find yourself reevaluating your relationships with friends and family who insist on giving your child loud and annoying toys (but try not to judge them too harshly!). Don't take electronic toys or books with sound effects on a car trip or on a plane. Noises that were cute the first five times will make you—and your fellow travelers—psychotic after the typical toddler's 1000-repetition cycle.

If your child has had frequent ear infections, have her hearing checked. Even a slight hearing loss can delay speech. A toddler who has started speaking and abruptly stops communicating should be evaluated by a professional. Ask your pediatrician for a referral.

SPECIAL PLAYS

Tapping into toddler humor can be as simple as a session of *yes* or *no* questions related to the book and pictures at hand. "Are YOU a hippopotamus?" "Do YOU bark like a dog?" Your toddler will find this hilarious, and you'll be teaching listening discrimination skills, categorization skills, and the difference between what's real and what's imaginary or funny.

One of the crucial skills your toddler is mastering at this stage is the ability to communicate with you. When she's trying to tell you something terribly important about her toddler world and you can't understand, she is likely to become frustrated. Be patient. Encourage her to repeat what she's said. Suggest that she use gestures or point to show you what she's talking about. Finger plays such as "Motor Boat, Motor Boat," in which the hand actions mimic the words, teach meaning and are very appealing to toddlers.

Compile a special photo album or scrapbook for your child with a single picture on each page. Spend time with your child going through the pictures, identifying family members, friends, and everyday objects. Ask, "Who's this?" and cue him with, "That's Grandpa." Include labels from favorite foods, portions of the packaging from new toys, pictures from magazines and catalogs, and greeting cards or postcards. Encourage him to use the book to communicate. For example, when he wants to go to the park, have him point to a picture of a park or playground equipment.

Use music to teach listening skills. You can either attend a toddler music class or introduce your child to favorites at home. Listen to music on the stereo, and dance together. Sing repetitive songs with hand motions, like "The Wheels on the Bus," "Head, Shoulders, Knees, and Toes," or "Twinkle, Twinkle Little Star." If you need to improve your repertoire of kid songs, check out some tapes and videos of children's songs. Your local library should have a selection of children's music.

Your toddler is able to process one- or two-step spoken commands. Set up an obstacle course in your living room. Direct your toddler to go under, over, in, around, through, or on various objects. This teaches him spatial concepts and reinforces his understanding of time and space. Also, giving him two-step commands like "Go under and through!" will help him build memory—not to mention coordination.

Take some time in the evening or at bedtime to talk about the events of the day. Use his scrapbook or photo album to review the highlights of his day. Talk about things he did or learned that make you proud to be his dad.

CALL FOR THE REFEREE

Your partner always tells your toddler what he wants and then gives it to him, like saying, "You're thirsty, here's some juice." You want him to ask for what he wants. It's time to start encouraging your son to start using his words. In fact, it is better for him to tell you than for you to tell him what he wants. Let him try, then repeat what you think he's saying, such as, "Do you want a cookie?" Or, if he wants to get out of his crib, encourage him to point or hold his arms up to let you know what he needs.

Your partner always uses "baby talk" with your son because she thinks it's cute. You think it sounds awful and you worry that he'll keep talking that way and people will laugh at him. It might be that the two of you are taking this too seriously. While it's true that it's best for children to hear accurate pronunciations, children quickly learn that each parent has a different style, and some family "codes," which baby talk often is, can be comforting. Children hear and model language from many sources. Relax, step back, and remember that both your toddler and your partner will grow out of the "baby talk" phase in time.

ADVICE FROM THE COACH

My child says no other words than "Da." He mostly grunts or points. What can I do to help him learn to talk? Why isn't he speaking yet? Okay, you're probably flattered by his choice of word, but let's do some detective work. First, how old is he? If he's only eighteen months old, he's not likely to be using many words yet. If he's two or older, you need to search for further clues, as two-year-olds are expected to have a handful of regularly used words. Your expectations for his speech may be based on other kids you know. Boys tend to speak later than girls, and only children are often behind younger siblings—who learn to speak simply to survive!

Pick up clues while observing him at play and interacting with your family. Does he seem to understand words? If not, get his hearing checked. If it's obvious that he's got the input systems working, consider what might be holding up the output. Does he have doting caregivers who anticipate his needs and wants? Let him ask for things. Offer him choices and wait to hear his answer. Does he have a shy, reserved personality? Use singing games and nursery rhymes to encourage speech. Is he the thoughtful type who's a little stumped on conversational topics? Use a toy phone for conversations with him. Put on a puppet show together. Use the exercises and Special Plays in this chapter to build the skills he needs to move on beyond that "Da."

I read about teaching toddlers sign language. Is this a good idea?
If you're willing to invest the time and energy into learning some basic sign language, it's certainly one way of helping your toddler communicate before she's mastered the spoken word. Books like *Baby Signs* by Linda Acredolo and *Sign with Your Baby* by Joseph Garcia are good resources if this is a route you want to take. Be warned, this will take some studying on your part. Sign language is a complex system, and one that Grandma and the babysitter may not be up on.

Rather than learning the whole language—and American Sign Language (ASL) is definitely a language unto itself—consider learning some basic signs. Just a few, like *eat, help, all alone,* and, of course, *Daddy,* will be enough to give your toddler a way to communicate her needs. As with most things toddler-related, repetition is key! You might find yourself signing *eat* for the millionth time, but after a million and one, your daughter will sign back.

If you would rather stick to the spoken word, that's perfectly fine. Barring any speech delays or other issues, your child will learn to speak eventually through everyday exposure to people talking.

My daughter is two and is stuttering; she just seems to have trouble getting the words out.
Being two is frustrating. She has a lot to say, but her mind is going faster than her mouth can move. Ignore the stuttering—she'll likely outgrow it in time. According to the American Academy of Pediatrics, repeating syllables, sounds, or words or hesitating between words is a common part of speech development in children. If the pattern continues for longer than two to three months and interferes with communication, then you should seek advice from her pediatrician on how best to proceed. In the meantime, do your best to ignore comments from other people about the stutter. You should try not to hurry her or finish sentences for her. Just slow down, give her your attention, and be patient.

My daughter whines. It's clear what she is saying, but I just don't know how to stop this constant whining. Sometimes she even screams to get my attention. What can I do to get her to stop?
I just know that somewhere in the Commandments there was an eleventh one stating, "Thou shalt not whine." Barring the discovery of that final Commandment, though, your best plan is to not respond to whining. Giving in to whining teaches your child that the whining works—which is definitely not what you're aiming for! Try using a calm tone of voice to say, "Please use your big-girl voice. I can't understand you." If the whining continues, repeat. Model the appropriate tone and tell her to use her "big-girl" voice. When she makes a positive effort to tone it down, respond accordingly.

As far as the screaming goes, earplugs are nice but not the best idea. If you fear for your eardrums—and some kids can pierce even the toughest ears—repeat the "inside voice" lesson. Toddlers scream for a variety of reasons, the first and most important being because they can. Toddlers also scream to get what they want. Don't fall for it, no matter how embarrassed or tired you are. As with the whining, if you reward the scream, she'll naturally figure ear-splitting shrieks are a good way to proceed.

My child seems to hear me, but she ignores me when I ask her to come here now or stop banging the block on the glass coffee table. She looks right at me but does not respond.

You're on track with simple, direct commands. But how much did she process? She obviously heard you, since she looked up, but to her it might have made as much sense as the teacher's voice on those old Charlie Brown specials: "Wahhh-wahh whhha whaaaa." Recognize that she may not understand your words, but ensure that you do get a response from her. Ignoring parents is a teenage skill, and not one that she should indulge in at her tender age. Move closer to her physically and illustrate the desired action while you repeat your request. Repeat twice, at most three times, but no more, or she will learn that she can ignore you the first twenty-five times. So when you say, "Stop banging the block," move closer and demonstrate by holding the block still. Once she has stopped, a diversionary tactic is in order. Help her stack blocks into an awesome tower. Now it's a win-win situation. You got the desired response, and she is enjoying time with you.

CHAPTER 3

Tantrums: Out of Bounds, No More Meltdowns

Once you had a baby happier than Randy Johnson pitching a no-hitter. Then one day, when it was time to leave the park, he totally blew his cool. Welcome to toddlerhood. Tantrums are rough on everybody, but they don't need to be a regular part of your life.

Toddlers like to think they're in control, even when they are not. A tantrum may just be your toddler's way of telling you he's frustrated things aren't going his way.

When you take the time to bring your child back from the edge of a meltdown, you are helping him develop self-control. He will learn that it's okay to get upset, but it's not okay to explode. Your toddler will model your behavior, so when he is in the car with you, don't curse the driver who cut you off. Take a deep breath, channel Yoda, and stay calm in the face of obvious irritation.

SO WHERE DO TANTRUMS COME FROM?

Tantrums typically occur between ages one and three. Once children learn to express themselves by talking, tantrums are a lot less frequent. They are a developmental stage, a sign that your toddler's nervous system is maturing and giving her an awareness of the world around her.

Toddlers have trouble identifying what they are feeling, and they lack the words to express themselves. New situations or people can throw off your toddler's sense of balance, too, and something as simple as leaving for day care can become a huge hassle. You might encounter the fearsome "Me do it" phase, where your toddler thinks she can do it on her own but isn't quite ready yet.

Her brain is also growing faster than her vocabulary, causing enormous frustration. Ever had something on the tip of your tongue but just couldn't get it out? Imagine doing that every day with every word you try to say, and you'll have some small sense of the communication challenges your toddler is facing.

Your toddler's sense of time is also skewed. There is no *later;* everything is *right now.* And if you miss the starter's gun, be prepared to deal with the immediate frustration.

Older toddlers are beginning to test the boundaries of *no.* They are learning just how far they can push the envelope, and it's your job to create the limits.

They are also more aware of their audience. They are trying to get your attention and get what they want. Think about

John McEnroe and some of his dramatic performances, and you will be inspired to curb this behavior now.

WATCH FOR TANTRUM TRIGGERS

You can figure out the signs that cause your own little slugger to start erupting. Try to see the world from his perspective. From your son's point of view, mascots, clowns, horses, Santa, or the Easter Bunny can be scary or risky and cause him to flip—and not in a good way.

Ever been shopping with your better half? Multiply your frustration by ten and you will appreciate how your toddler feels. Let him know where you're going and what you're doing, before you go and while you're on the way there. He'll feel part of the team if you let him in on your game plan.

Run errands in the morning, far enough before naptime that he won't be tired out. Afternoons are a difficult time for most toddlers and are best saved for playing. And allow plenty of time for whatever is scheduled—too much, too fast is a recipe for crankiness.

Sometimes big events like birthdays, holidays, vacations, or parties can make toddlers more prone to tantrums. Illness and lack of sleep can also trigger trouble. Watch out for tantrums in the making, and help your child try to deal with these unavoidable disruptions.

Any break in routine can be difficult for your toddler. Toddlers need life to be predictable. This doesn't mean you can't run off to the park or zoo, but prepare him ahead of time for the change in schedule. Warn him when you're getting ready to end an activity. A five-minute warning, followed by three- and one-minute warnings, can help him understand that change is coming.

STAND YOUR GROUND

The best way to keep tantrums at bay is to not give your toddler what he wants if he's screaming for it. Giving in means the tantrum worked, and your toddler will keep punching the same buttons. As long as he's not in pain or true distress (and yes, you will learn to tell the difference), avoid giving in while he's kicking and screaming.

ANATOMY OF A TANTRUM

It sometimes seems like tantrums come straight out of left field, but there's always a lead-up. Tantrums often begin with the "I'm unhappy and cranky" stage. At this point you can sense a slow burn coming on—his voice starts to get louder, he begins repeating himself, or he shuts his eyes.

Then he might start kicking, stomping his feet, or making his hands into fists. Here's where his favorite word, *NO*, comes into play with a vengeance. That's the warning flag for danger ahead. Now he'll refuse to follow your directions and ignore your requests for him to stop. The next step is a full-blown tantrum.

At this point, it can be harder to prevent a complete melt-down than stopping a quarterback with the ball on the one-yard line. Once things have escalated to the kicking, biting, screaming, and head-banging stage, it's every man for himself. All you can do at that point is damage control.

GET AHEAD OF THE CURVE

The trick is to catch the tantrum before the full-scale fireworks. Before you have reached the point of no return, here are some things to try.

Acknowledge his frustration or bad mood. Get down to his level and talk to him. Using words to help describe what he's feeling can help him voice his frustration and may slow down the burn. Everyday emotions like fear and disappointment can cause your toddler to erupt. If he's ready to go ballistic because you couldn't find his favorite book, give him words to express himself. Say, "I know you are really sad we can't find your book. I'm sure that's frustrating for you." Offer an alternative. Go on a hunt for the book together, or ask him if there is another book you can read together. If he's afraid of something, like being left at day care or with the babysitter, help him express that fear, reassure him that you (or Mom) will be back to pick him up, and leave. It may be hard, but he will learn that he's safe and that you will be back.

Grab a drink or snack to break the chain of events. Distraction is a wonderful tool. It may seem underhanded, but toddlers are fickle. The offer of a few handy Goldfish crackers has kept many a surly toddler from the brink of disaster.

If you're still in the "I'm unhappy" stage of the tantrum, remember: a hungry, thirsty, tired, or overexcited toddler will melt down faster than Andrew Agassi after a bad line call.

Offer your cranky toddler a cool drink of water, a snack, or a cuddle with one of her favorite books—she may even fall asleep in your lap just like she did when she was "little." Try holding her on your lap and rubbing her back or stroking her arms. Physical reassurance can be calming.

With older toddlers, try appealing to the desire to be a big kid, such as saying something like, "Where's my big girl?" Or "Can you ask me in your big-girl voice?" Try offering an incentive to help her pull herself together. For example, "When you calm down, we can read a story or play a game."

Flexibility is the key. Every child changes moods differently, and your playbook has to reflect that.

DAMAGE CONTROL

If your toddler has truly reached the end of his rope, you may be at the point of no return. At this stage he might be thrashing on the floor in full-scale hysteria, screeching. If you're lucky, he's only doing this for an audience of one, but be prepared to deal with this behavior in places like your local hardware store.

The first, and most important, rule is to KEEP COOL. Now is not the time to see who can scream the loudest. Yelling and threats are useless, and won't change your child's behavior for the better. Put-downs are no improvement. This is just a developmental phase, not a permanent part of your child's personality. This, too, shall pass—just like the loose change he swallowed last week.

Keep your eye on him. You can step away if you need to, but know that it's scary for kids to have tantrums. They're spinning out of control and don't know how to stop all by themselves. Often, what will help more is coming to him after a moment or two, giving some hugs, and letting him collapse into tears on your shoulder.

If necessary, take it outside. Even if it means leaving a store without finishing your errand, cut your losses and leave the situation. If your toddler is screaming for a treat or item from the store, this will teach him you mean it when you say no. Alternatively, leaving may be a relief to him, as the stimulation of new places and things could be contributing to the tantrum in ways not obvious to your adult eyes.

"Tackle Time"

Thirteen months to three years

This activity promotes learning how to ramp down out-of-control emotions and physical aggression. Every kid needs to know how to simmer down and take it to the mat.

- Place your child on or near an inflatable toy.
- Encourage your child to blow off steam by pushing and wrestling with the toy, cheered on by Dad.
- For kids over two, get the kind of toy you put water in at the base, for great weight resistance. That way, they can push it while standing up.

Game tip: *Use the toy to redirect your child. You can say, "If you are mad, we can hit this toy. We don't hit people."*

"Lion Tamer"

One to three years

Help bully-proof your child and tell others to back off. This is a great activity if your child is a little bit shy.

• Hold a stuffed lion and roar, starting out at a low level.
• Have your kid say "Shhh" or "Stop."
• As the game progresses, get louder and taller.

Game tip: This is a fun activity for a kid who needs to let off steam. It is especially good for helping a shy child learn to be assertive.

"Pillow Fight"

Fifteen months to three years

Get a jump on your child's ability to stand up for himself with other children. This will help him handle excitement and frustration, something we all can use.

- Take some soft pillows and show him how to bop Dad. Then bop him back.
- Fall over and tell your child how strong he is.
- If your child hits too hard, caution him, "This is just for fun."

Game tip: *This can be a tough game for kids to keep in control. Take it slow, and ramp it up carefully.*

"Sidelined"

Fifteen months to three years

Defuse a meltdown and bring your player back to the game with some R&R with the coach.

• Take your child aside and tell him you understand he is upset.
• Briefly describe the situation that caused the upset. "You are mad because . . ."
• Reassure your child and calmly say, "You are okay, pull yourself together."
• Put your arm around your child or pat him on the back.

Game tip: *Sometimes a change of place or new activity can help a child feel better.*

"Mad Game Workout"

Two to three years

Here's a winning game to show your child how to get mad without having to hit, scream, or kick when she is upset.

• Say, "Mad, mad, mad" in a "mad" but not-too-loud voice.
• Illustrate through your facial expressions that you are mad.
• Say, "Grrrrrrr, I'm frustrated."
• Prompt your child to copy what you do.

Game tip: Use puppets or stuffed animals and act out real-life situations that make you or your child mad or frustrated.

"First Aid for Dad"

Two to three years

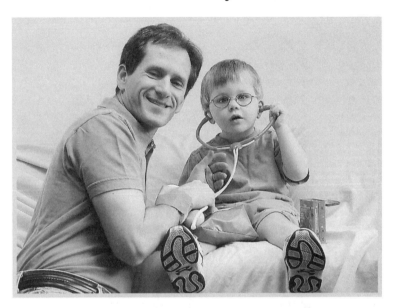

Some tantrum-prevention plays before your child's next visit to the doctor—often a scary event for toddlers.

- Purchase a plastic doctor's kit at a toy store.
- Ask, "Do you want to listen to my heart?" Help him select and use the stethoscope.
- Say, "Now let's look in Dad's ear."
- Request that he check your hands, leg, foot, etc.
- Use a couple of real Band-Aids from the medicine cabinet.
- Use stuffed animals as patients.

Game tip: *Keep the box of Band-Aids in the cabinet, or you'll end up using the whole box.*

"Daddy Tosses a Tantrum"

Two to three years

Demonstrate through your own play-acting what a tantrum looks like. This helps your child see emotions through the eyes of others.

• Say, "Daddy is mad."
• Lie down on the floor and quietly throw a tantrum.
• Using humor, pretend to whine or be mad and say, "Daddy can use words when he is mad."
• Use words to name feelings. "I'm mad, I have a mad face."
• Pretend a toy is having a tantrum, and help it calm down.

Game tip: *This can be a scary game, so go slowly and speak quietly. Toddlers aren't sure of the differences between reality and pretend.*

TIPS FOR WINNING

Limit choices—don't make your child pick from a zillion flavors of ice cream or ten pairs of pants; two is plenty to choose from. Too many choices can cause confusion and frustration. Bypass toddler angst by making decisions simple.

Remember that two errands per outing are about all your child can handle. Resist the temptation to get everything done in one day. Those days are gone, and you may as well relax and go with it.

If your kid hits you—and every parent gets socked, or even head-butted, once in a while—don't hit back. Instead, yelp loudly and say, "That hurts."

Try to redirect your child when you see the windup to a tantrum. Offer incentives for positive behavior—reading a story, playing airplane, getting twirled around.

Focus on your child when he's behaving like the player you know he is, and he will take pride in the attention he's getting.

Prevent tantrums from the get-go by stashing bottles of water and snacks in the car, diaper bag, and stroller to keep a hungry or thirsty child from getting meaner than Dennis Rodman on a bad-hair day.

SAFETY ZONE

If your kid is trying to kick or hit, hold him sideways. Let him work out some of the frustration. You can even tell him that he is having trouble controlling himself, so you are helping him.

If you are on the edge—and it's amazing how someone who barely reaches your knees can push you there—take a step back. Tell your child, "I can't talk to you right now. Daddy needs to calm down." Walk away before you commit unsportsmanlike conduct.

Some kids will trash their rooms when they are having a tantrum. Others will actually bang their heads on the walls or the floor if they are left to rage. Supervision is your best bet. One option is to wrap your arms around your child and help him contain his anger. Another option is to stay in the room with him to prevent any major damage—to himself or his surroundings.

Kitchens and bathrooms don't mix with a toddler throwing a tantrum. If you feel the surroundings are unsafe, take your toddler into a room that has fewer hazards.

SPECIAL PLAYS

Sing a song that describes going away to help prepare a child for leaving: "Bye-bye park, bye-bye park . . . we'll come back soon . . ." *Bye-bye* is a great toddler word and can be used to ease transitions for just about everything.

Use a puppet or stuffed animal and act out getting upset and calming down, showing your child through play how to handle frustration and anger. Make up stories about the puppets or animals, illustrating specific situations in which the main character resolves conflict without hitting or screaming. For example, "Once upon a time, there was a little boy named _____ at day care and the puppy took his toy and wouldn't give it back . . ."

CALL FOR THE REFEREE

Dads and moms are at each other's throats when their little goalie does her best imitation of a British soccer hooligan. Yelling at each other won't solve the disagreement or fix the tantrum. Everyone feels pretty worked up when they have a screaming toddler on their hands. It works best if partners stay united, or the toddlers will conquer. They can smell fear, you know! Discuss consequences with your partner ahead of time and come up with some consequences you both can agree to.

Your toddler throws an incredible ear-splitting tantrum. You and your partner disagree about how to handle the situation. In most cases, bad attention is more fun than no attention at all. One way to eliminate negative behavior is not to yell or spank but to ignore the behavior altogether. Listen without letting him know that you're paying attention, and as he calms down, suggest some fun activity—playing a game, having a drink of water, etc. He'll learn that tantrums get him nowhere, while good behavior earns rewards. (Unless he's an NBA star, and he's not tall enough to worry about that yet.)

Your son totally goes into a meltdown when Mom leaves. Toddlers don't understand how time works and might be fearful Mom isn't coming back. Make Daddy time cool time, doing things Mom doesn't do. Fill a couple of spray bottles with water and squirt them in the sink or at the plants outside, or get out a flashlight and make pictures on the walls with light and shadows.

ADVICE FROM THE COACH

Every grocery store checkout lane is filled with toys, candy, or other junk! I don't know how to handle the nagging or the flood of tears when I don't give in.

Don't you love the marketing folks? They know when you're at your weakest. After a seemingly endless struggle to keep the Frosted Sugar Bombs out of the cart, here you are, almost to the finish line, and there's a gauntlet of toys and treats. This is where advance planning comes in handy. Set clear expectations with your toddler. Let him know today is not a "treat" day. Beware of saying, "Next time," because kids have memories like elephants when it comes to treats. He *will* call you on it next time. Bring a snack and a toy to whip out at the critical moment. Above all, be strong! Giving in "just this once" will turn into a million more "just this once" moments if you let the nagging and tears break through your resolve. He will get distracted with something else soon enough; you just need to wait it out.

When we went out for ice cream, the shop was out of rainbow sherbet. I tried to buy her lime, but my little girl threw herself on the floor and had a huge tantrum! I'm not sure if I'll ever take her out again.

In toddler time, there will never be another opportunity to have rainbow sherbet. Offering some limited choices can help. Next time, tell her she can have vanilla or chocolate (if the rainbow sherbet is still out of stock, or she's dead-set on another missing flavor). If the choices aren't working and she starts to melt down, tell her *she* can choose a flavor or you can leave. Still inconsolable? Time to go. Take her home immediately and she will rapidly figure out that screaming won't get her where she wants to be—eating some ice cream with Dad. The key is to remain calm even in the face of toddler meltdown.

When it's time to leave the park after playing, my son FLIPS OUT. He screams, grabs on to the equipment, and makes a huge scene. I dread taking him there.

Transitions are tough for toddlers. If you're making a change from one place to the next—say the park to the car—you need to give plenty of warning so he can get used to the idea. Try something like, "We'll have five more pushes on the swing." Give him time warnings such as "Five more minutes" and "One more minute." If possible, you might try taking something with you from the park, like some leaves or a rock (too large to swallow). This can help him switch gears by letting him keep a connection with the place he is leaving, without your needing to pitch a tent on the grass.

When my son is ticked off, he trashes his room. He dumps out his drawers and throws his books and toys around. My partner is at her wits' end.

Sometimes it's all we can do to keep ourselves from running from the house screaming. Before you freak out the neighbors, though, you need to realize that your toddler simply doesn't have control of his feelings yet. Take a deep breath. Try eliminating some of the clutter in his room. Fewer toys will mean fewer things to throw on the floor. If he continues to trash his room, make sure he has to help clean it up every time. It will take repeating, but he will eventually get the message that he has to clean up his own messes. Eventually he will even take that a step further and realize it's easier to not make the mess in the first place.

What should we do when we're at Grandma's and my kid keeps going for the remote and breakables and creates a big scene? Grandma says she would never have put up with this behavior!

Grandparents can have pretty selective memories when it comes to their parenting skills and practices. For kids under two, remote controls, keys, and knickknacks are irresistible. The best-case scenario is to call Grandma ahead of time and tell her to put away the china cherubs, remote controls, and other baby bait—or do this yourself once you get there. Bring along toys for your child to play with, or leave some special toys at the grandparents' home. If Grandma isn't willing to play along by making the environment more toddler friendly, you may suggest that either she should come to your place or you should meet on neutral, kid-friendly turf (like a park). Your kid's magnetic attraction to breakables will gradually go away, and then Grandma's house can be a play zone again.

If someone touches our little guy's special toys or blanket, he goes berserk. This makes playing with friends or going to the church nursery a HUGE pain in the you-know-what.

Lots of kids, especially boys, can be really territorial. Toddlers can't share, and you can't make it happen. You can tell him he doesn't have to share what's most special, like his blanket—then leave it home or put it up out of reach if a friend is coming over. Out of sight, out of mind!

My child is terrified of going to the doctor. He screams as soon as we drive up and makes a huge spectacle in the waiting room. It makes me want to yell, too!

Do you look forward to getting poked and prodded by a stranger? If you weren't paying for it, you'd probably call the police. As far as he's concerned, visiting the doctor is likely to involve either feeling sick or getting a shot—two less-than-happy perks of being a kid.

You can ease his fears by rehearsing what happens at the doctor's office, so he has some sense of what to expect. Read some children's books about doctor visits. Buy a toy doctor's kit, throw in a few Band-Aids, and let him practice "fixing" his stuffed animals. Pretend he's the doctor and let him listen to their "hearts," bandage their paws, and examine their eyes and ears. You may end up playing this until you're so sick of it that getting a tetanus shot feels like fun in comparison.

Praise your toddler when he gets through an appointment without a tantrum. Also, try to make time to do something fun immediately after going to the doctor, such as going to the park, getting some ice cream, or going to the toy store. Give your toddler a chance to tell you his "story" about his adventure in the doctor's office.

CHAPTER 4

The Twilight Zone: In Search of Sleep

Three of the sexiest words you can whisper in Mom's ear are "The baby's asleep!" Toddlers often wake up several times a night, and unless they have learned to soothe themselves, they have trouble going back to sleep on their own, regardless of where they sleep. They don't like to wake up alone (who does?) and may need a little physical contact to relax and get back to sleep. A crib can be a big, empty place when you're in a room all by yourself. Some parents are lucky. The baby, for whatever reason, is a sound sleeper and grows into a toddler who not only goes to bed on his own, but also sleeps all night. Then there are the rest of us.

You've had your entire life to get used to sleeping. All your toddler knows when she wakes up in the middle of the night, especially if she's in a crib, is that she's in a padded cell with bars, and it's very dark. If that was your experience, what would you do? That knowledge might help you keep your sanity when it's 2:38 A.M. and you're trying to get your eighteen-month-old back to sleep for the third time that night. Somewhere out there is another parent trying to do exactly the same thing.

THE TODDLER SLEEP CYCLE

Night waking is a normal part of every human's sleep cycle. The difference between your toddler's sleep and yours is that long ago, you learned how to wake up and drift right back to sleep. In fact, when you glance at the clock and notice that it's 2 A.M. and you have half the night to continue sleeping, you're probably overjoyed. Your toddler, on the other hand, wakes up and has no clue what's going on. And he may have become used to certain comforts—like nursing or rocking—and hasn't evolved to a point where he can go back to sleep *without* those things. The goal here is to get him used to the idea of falling asleep on his own.

If you're getting desperate, try holding onto a soft, small stuffed animal or blanket when you're cuddling with your toddler. This will help transfer your smell to the stuffed animal, which will comfort your toddler when you're not there with him. Put this transition item to bed with him for naps and at night. With any luck, this favorite item will help him get back to sleep when he wakes up in the middle of the night. And if you're sensing that this is all about luck, you're partially correct.

STEPS TOWARD A PEACEFUL NIGHT'S SLEEP

If you look like you're having a blast before bedtime, your son or daughter isn't going to want to miss out on the fun. So it's time to make the house calm and peaceful—or at least create that illusion. It's better if the TV isn't playing anywhere that your child can see or hear it. If there's music, make it low-key. If your spouse is putting your child to bed, you might want to look like you're going to be heading there soon yourself. In other words, think of the policeman motioning people away when a raging fire is going on in the background: "There's nothing to see here, folks, nothing to see." The idea is to offer your child as little stimulation as possible and send the message that it's time to calm down.

Meanwhile, the family should have a nighttime routine. Try to do things the same way every evening. As you probably know, kids love predictability, and guess what? So do toddlers. They thrive on it. They want to know what's coming next, that they're going to be brushing their teeth and not being whisked off to the dentist, and that they're going to be climbing into bed instead of an SUV. And so a basic bedtime routine might be something like this: bath and pajamas; brush teeth; read a book; hugs and good-night kisses. The whole operation should take no more than half an hour, and if you do it right, your child will be nodding off by the end of each bedtime session. The problem is, this doesn't happen overnight, or even over several nights. Like any new skill, she won't learn this instantly, and you have to be prepared to work at it.

So just like you would troubleshoot with a conked-out computer, check out this troubleshooting guide and see if you need to consider employing some of these strategies:

- *R&R time together.* You can't just toss your kid into the bed and say, "So long. Don't forget to write." So sit your toddler in your lap and read a story—or make one up. Rock together or snuggle on the bed. Body contact will relax your toddler and help him drift off. Obviously, though, don't get too comfortable with this routine. The ultimate objective is to make this a non-contact sport. At the beginning, if your child's in a bed that can fit an adult, you could start off by lying down with him. In theory, several nights later, you'll be sitting on the bed, patting your child on the back, or tapping his foot, or just sitting there quietly. Eventually, as that works well, you up the ante and you take a chair next to the bed. Before you know it, you're way across the room, and at some point, you're in Guam.

- *Avoid late-night hunger pangs.* Do you keep forgetting to give your daughter a snack? Not to worry. You can give her one when she wakes you up at 1 A.M. Seriously, though, it's smart to refuel your child about thirty minutes before bed with a protein-rich snack like yogurt, cheese and crackers, or pudding. Even a piece of turkey can help.

- *Dress for comfort.* Be sure sleepers or pajamas are comfortable (not too loose or too tight). If your toddler has cold feet, you might want to consider letting him sleep in pajamas with feet or else with socks, because chances are that blanket's going to come off at night. And you don't want to create any reason—like a chilly room—to jolt your child out of sleep.

• *Check out the bedroom.* Your toddler needs the best sleeping conditions possible. That could include room-darkening shades or a night-light—whichever seems necessary. Some need both—shades to cut out streetlights and early morning sunlight (as well as scary shadows) and a night-light for comfort. You also might want to consider installing a baby gate on your toddler's door and leaving the door open. This will keep him safely corralled and still connected, rather than feeling like he's being shut away from the family come bedtime. Kids also overheat easily and sleep best in a cooler room, between 60 and 65 degrees.

• *Try some music.* Take a tip from day-care providers who put children down for naps every day. Light classical, easy listening, and nature sounds all have soothing qualities. Keep the volume low. Some kids like to have a music box wound up to lull them to sleep.

• *Keep a favorite stuffed animal around.* Some toddlers need that special friend to help them drift off to sleep. If that works for your toddler, you're going to consider that ragged stuffed bunny your special friend, too.

GETTING BACK TO SLEEP

A toddler who has barely woken up and seems groggy can sometimes be soothed back to dreamland if you simply rub his back and whisper, "You're okay. Go back to sleep." In order to not rouse your child awake, keep your conversation to a minimum. Avoid making direct eye contact.

If she's a little more awake, you need to collect your thoughts and be okay with the fact that it's 3 A.M. and this is going to take longer than you hoped. Sit down and hold her hand through the crib, or rub her back for five minutes. Repeat softly. "It's okay. Time to sleep." Whatever your approach, try to keep her in bed, since picking her up might wake her up more. You can try hugging her if she's standing up in the crib—again, without picking her up—and letting her know you're there and that you love her, but it's still sleeptime. Use your instincts on this one. If leaving her in bed when she's crying feels wrong, then don't do it. Some parents, especially if the child is pretty young, feel that letting a child cry herself to sleep is a good option, one that will teach the toddler to fall asleep on her own. But there really are no rules. If there were, we'd all use them, and they would work, and we wouldn't need chapters in books like this. Unfortunately, parenting—especially when it comes to getting a toddler to sleep—is a series of educated guesswork.

Some quick scenarios to think about, if your child is awake at the midnight hour and you can't figure out why:

• For starters, maybe your child is awake because there's a scent wafting through the air—right, did you check her diaper? Better do that.

• Feel your child's forehead. Is she sick? Uh-oh. Well, it may be time to wake up your spouse and have both of you swing into action, one parent comforting your daughter while the other goes for a thermometer.

- Has her blanket fallen off the bed, or if she has a pacifier or that favorite nighttime toy, could that have slipped out of the crib?

- There could be a dozen more reasons why your child is awake. A baby monitor, especially one with a video, is a great tool. Sometimes your child might just be crying in her sleep, moaning but about to drift back into oblivion. By rushing in with no clue what's going on, you might actually wake your child and cause you both to be up for the next couple of hours.

THE BIG MOVE—OUT OF YOUR BED AND INTO THEIRS

First of all, if your toddler is sleeping with you and your spouse, you're not alone. Don't feel terrible. Other parents do it. You're not weak. That said, it's a habit that's difficult to break, so if you never got into this practice, good for you. If your toddler is sharing your bed, the time has come to reclaim the mattress for yourself and your partner.

While separation anxiety tends to peak between ages one and two, this is, ironically, a good time to teach your child how to sleep alone. She is likely to kick up a much bigger fuss after age two, so it is definitely worth the effort to do something now, before all is lost and your child is someday thirty-two years old and in therapy because she was still sleeping with her parents at nineteen. Okay, that's a little over the top, but you see where I'm going. The most peaceful way to make this transition is over the course of a few weeks, or even a few months. If you're feeling short on patience, there are a variety of ways to handle this—some quicker than others.

One possibility is to place a mattress on the floor by your bed. It's a possibility that some parents employ, but I don't recommend it. What self-respecting toddler is going to remain on that mattress when he could scale up to his parents' bed?

If your toddler has been sleeping in a crib in your room, you can try the "migrating crib" technique. Over the course of a few nights, move the crib farther away from your bed. This gets your toddler used to the idea of sleeping "away" from you. The next step is to move the crib into your child's new bedroom. That baby monitor can help in responding when she needs you.

But the quickest route to getting your toddler to sleep in her own bed is to put her there. Let her fall asleep with you in the room, and sneak out quietly. Be prepared for a few trips back and forth while your toddler gets used to the idea of waking up in her own room. This will go more smoothly if you spend some time during the day letting her explore her crib in its new surroundings. If she isn't taking daytime naps in her crib or bed, this is the time to start.

MOVING FROM A CRIB TO A "BIG-KID" BED

A good rule of thumb is to go by your toddler's size in relation to his crib. With the crib mattress at the lowest it will go, if your child's chest is above the top of the railing, it's definitely time to make the switch. At this stage, your little climber may feel inspired to get his leg over the railing—and your imagination can do the rest.

If you and your partner have decided he's ready for the move, you'll need to take a few steps to ease the transition. If there are other big changes happening in your family—like a move, a new sibling on the way, or anything that disturbs the norm—it may not be the best time to make the change. Try to pick a time when the rest of your toddler's life is going pretty smoothly.

Rather than expecting your toddler to spend his very first night in his new bed, start with naps. Give him a little time to adjust to the idea. It helps if you're talking about the bed days or weeks before it suddenly magically appears in his room. And no matter what, he'll get out of bed a lot at first. Have patience and cheerfully take him back and settle him down.

OUT OF BED AGAIN?

If your toddler keeps popping out of his room, a gate across the doorway can keep him from roaming around, while giving him the security he needs by letting him see what's happening outside his door. If there are stairs in your house then you obviously, absolutely will want a gate, if not at the doorway, then in the hall before the steps. A toddler roaming while you're asleep can get hurt all too easily.

If he escapes the confines of his bed and his room, return him immediately with very little fanfare. What you don't need is your toddler giggling and deciding that leaving the bedroom and outwitting Daddy is a terrific game—one he wants to play over and over. Tell him, "Shhh, it's bedtime," without turning on any lights. Night-lights provide safe illumination.

When you're exhausted common sense often goes out the window, but don't break out a book in the middle of the night to calm your child down, or take your little girl to the family room to let her play and tire herself out again. You'll just teach her that all exits from her bedroom lead to playtime, no matter what the time. You may end up putting your son or daughter back to bed several times in one night, and many nights in a row, but he or she *will* learn to stay in bed. Eventually. Really.

NO MONSTERS ALLOWED

This is the age where kids start to have—and remember even after waking up—nightmares. Shadows can look pretty sinister, and monsters may begin popping up from under the bed or out of the closet, or from the outside when a car backfires or a dog barks. Unfortunately, telling her there are no such things as monsters won't make them go away. In your toddler's mind, those monsters are as real as you are. You might be tempted to pretend that you agree with her and show her how you're scaring the monsters away. But as cool as it might feel to play the hero, that can easily backfire and teach your child that monsters *do* exist, and that once you leave, they just might come back to finish their job. It's better to just be calmly insistent that everything is okay, that monsters don't exist, and we lock the doors every night so no one can get in.

TOUCHDOWN!

As noted earlier, some parents are lucky; getting a toddler to sleep is relatively easy, and going from a crib to sleeping soundly in a big-kid bed is hardly difficult at all. Other parents wind up spending a fortune at Starbucks, downing lattes in the hopes of staying awake enough to make it to the next day. But be encouraged that a good night's rest for you, your partner, and your toddler will happen one of these days if you keep at it. And once you are there, make the most of your time with your significant other. Before you know it, she'll be pregnant, and soon you can do this all over again!

Don't be caught with your pants (or pajamas) down. Now is a good time to put a lock on your bedroom door to avoid having your toddler walk in during a romantic moment. But you're not a fortress. If you always have the door locked, you risk sending the message "We don't want you" to your toddler, and you also are creating an element of danger. If your toddler is roaming around at night, you want him or her waking you up, difficult as that is to believe.

"In the Clinch with Coach"

One to three years

*G*etting some Dad contact just before bed is a great way to connect. This activity builds the basic connection between you and your child, and reinforces the bedtime ritual.

• Put your hands on your kid's shoulders.
• Give your toddler a hug and plant a smooch.
• Say, "I love you, you're a great kid!"

Game tip: *Make this your last step in going to bed.*

"Down for the Count"

One to two and a half years

Get into the clinch and take a halftime break on the couch with Coach's favorite little player.

- Get comfy on the couch or in Dad's big chair.
- Say, "I like being your dad."

Game tip: *Sing your favorite song or name your favorite team.*

"Wake-up Call"

One to three years

Looking for some more shut-eye on a Saturday morning?

- Drag yourself out of bed, then give your child some milk in a cup or bottle.
- Get out some books or a video and hope for the best.

Game tip: *Kids are great at opening doors and even unlocking doors to the outside. Consider gating your child's bedroom door if you don't want to find him outside.*

"Out of Bounds"

Two to three years

Sleeping alone in the dark can be scary. Playing in a dark tent with Dad can help your little player get over fears and night-time fussing. This can also help make the transition into sleep easier.

Game tip: *Look for small children's flashlights which turn off after the toddler has gone to sleep to preserve the batteries. Find toys, aquariums, or a light show to keep your child company at night and promote relaxation and sleep.*

"Reading the Stats with Dad"

One to three years

Kids' brains take in more information when reading is a contact sport. Rocking or sitting with Dad promotes a sense of security and helps everyone wind down for sleep.

• Sit with your toddler on your lap.
• Read a book about going to bed, like *Goodnight Moon*.
• Count the pages in the book.
• After the book is over say, "Now it's time for bed."

Game tip: *Body contact helps lower the heart rate and helps your kid sleep longer and more deeply.*

"Touchdown"

One to three years

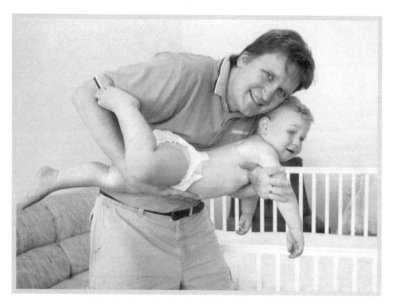

Help your child slip into sleeptime. This game will land your "ace pilot" in his nighttime hangar.

- Lift your child gently around his chest and make zoom noises.
- Make him fly, lifting him up and down.
- The "plane" arrives in the bedroom and Dad announces, "Time for landing."
- Place the child into bed.
- Sing a good-night song, counting, "One little, two little, three little airplanes."

Game tip: *Stop sometimes and encourage the copilot to say, "Go and stop."*

"Power Nap/Team Sleep"

One to three years

Here's the reason you tell your partner you need a big-screen plasma TV.

• Give Mom a night out or a Saturday to shop. Dad can hang out with his rookie and take a nap or watch a game.
• Buddy up and intertwine your fingers with your child's, holding hands together.
• Talk about what is happening during the game. Hang out.

Game tip: *Tell your child a story about a favorite game you liked to play when you were a child, or sing a favorite song.*

"Flashlight Good Night"

Eighteen months to three years

Both toddlers and dads need help winding down after a busy day. Following the light builds a connection between language and memory in your child's brain.

- Buy one of the many flashlights for children that can change color.
- For kids under two, Dad directs the light on items in the bedroom.
- Say, "Good night window, good night bed, good night closet."
- Using the flashlight, draw shapes and lines vertically and horizontally.
- Once your child is two, he can turn the flashlight on and find objects in the room.

- You can play tag, catching each other, if both of you have lights.
- Practice counting stuffed animals, books, or toys in your child's room.

Game tip: *After Dad has tucked him in, he can use the flashlight as a night-light.*

TIPS FOR WINNING

To encourage sleeping through the night, and to make bedtime easier, try to keep daytime naps to around one to two hours.

Put big family pictures on the walls by your child's bed or beside his crib. Seeing familiar faces can help alleviate some of the fear of being alone that hits hardest at sleeptime.

Avoid watching the evening news, pro wrestling, and other loud and disturbing television programs with your child, especially before bedtime. It's too much for a toddler and will affect his sleep. Try to look at what you're viewing from the perspective of a toddler, who sees people in a car chase on TV and thinks it's not only real but also could come leaping out of the TV and into the living room at any moment. Give peace and quiet a chance, especially when you're trying to get your toddler to sleep.

To calm down a kid who doesn't want to slow down and sleep, try sitting at the window and counting cars going by, if there's traffic on the road where you live. You can also count parked cars, stars, trees, or whatever happens to be in your line of sight.

If your toddler wakes up, don't wait until he's pounding on his bedroom door to be let out. Use your baby monitor. You will learn how to recognize the noise of a toddler who is just turning in his sleep, and one who is getting ready to vault out of bed. It is a whole lot easier to get him back to sleep before he gets out of bed.

THE SAFETY ZONE

A kid this age doesn't need pillows or big stuffed animals in her bed. Stacked pillows and animals can become makeshift stairs—all the better to escape from the crib! One or two small stuffed animals, or a cloth book, will be enough to entertain your little Houdini—without becoming props in her next disappearing act.

Keep those outside doors locked. Once kids are mobile they can walk right outside—into snow or rain, traffic, and trouble. Many is the story I've heard of a pajama-clad toddler prancing down the middle of the road, only to be returned home by a neighbor—to parents who swear up and down that Junior was sound asleep in bed. A dead bolt, and possibly even a chain lock, on your outside door is a very good thing.

Toddlers can fall out of big-kid beds. Side rails can increase your toddler's sense of security when going to sleep, and they also make sleeping much safer. If you're staying over in an unfamiliar bed, place the mattress on the floor, or push the bed against a wall and use a pillow barricade on the other side.

Even if you're on the last errand of the day, if your toddler falls asleep in the car seat, it is important that you not leave her sleeping alone in the car while you run in somewhere. Better to save the errand for another day or wake her and take her in with you. The wrath of a wakened toddler is far preferable to the anguish you would feel if something happened to her while you were away from the car.

Lower the crib mattress after your child learns to stand. It's one simple thing you can do to keep her in her crib and out of the doctor's office.

A child under the age of six shouldn't sleep, or play, on the top bunk of a bunk bed. He may think he can fly, but gravity will be a big downer when he tries it from the top bunk. Save yourself the fun of explaining the leg cast on your toddler to your mother-in-law, and make the bunk bed out of bounds for now.

Put locks and window guards on windows. Regular screens won't keep a kid from falling out—this is a major cause of injuries in small children. Be sure to place your toddler's bed away from the window in his room. Removing the temptation is half the battle.

Be aware of any loose or looped window-blind cords in your child's room. These are strangulation hazards and need to be eliminated completely or tacked way out of your child's reach. Again, place your child's crib or bed as far from the window as possible. The Window Covering Safety Council (associated with the Consumer Products Safety Commission) provides a free fix-it kit for window blinds, and can be reached at 1-800-506-4636.

SPECIAL PLAYS

Have good night songs, and put them on tape. You don't have to be a trained singer. Your toddler will like hearing your voice, and the songs or stories will help soothe her to sleep.

Try making shadow animals on the walls—bunnies, dogs, birds, or whatever your imagination provides. Dads often have a talent for this—it must come attached with the Y chromosome. Use your imagination and the shadows to tell your toddler a sleep-friendly story.

Use soothing crib toys that imitate aquariums or make light patterns. Lamps that have revolving filters with colors and pictures can be good in the room. You can also try sticking glow-in-the-dark stars over his bed. Kids often need something to watch if they wake up or as they go to sleep.

Have your child help put favorite dolls or stuffed animals "to bed," covering them up and singing your favorite lullaby all the while. You can also say "night-night" to the house and objects in her room. Think *Goodnight Moon*, the home version.

CALL FOR THE REFEREE

Agreeing on how you and your partner are going to teach your toddler good sleep habits can take time and patience. You'll need to come to some agreement, as this is yet another case where consistency—and patience—are important. You might be woken up by a drooling kiss in the middle of the night for the umpteenth time and catch yourself mumbling something about, "Not tonight, honey," when reality sinks in. Just get up, help your toddler back to bed, and remember that someday he'll be away at college and you'll wish he were toddling down the hall in his pajamas to wake you up.

Your toddler wakes up during the night and you can't agree on what to do. There's nothing like several nights of interrupted sleep to make even the most even-keeled parent turn into someone resembling Mike Tyson after losing a fight. Don't try to hash things out during the night, when you are both ready to throw a sharp left hook at the next person who pops off. Talk about your approach during the day, when everyone is feeling reasonably civil.

Your partner always seems to give in when your toddler cries and wants another "night-night kiss." You think he needs to just settle down and go to sleep. Kids are much more likely to go back to sleep if Dad steps up to the plate when the child wakes up.

ADVICE FROM THE COACH

I can sleep through anything. My partner complains I won't get up, but honestly, I'm dead to the world and don't hear a thing.

Two words: baby monitor. Just because your kid is out of infancy doesn't mean monitors aren't still useful. Crank it up and stick it on *your* nightstand. You can always ask your partner to nudge you in the ribs if you're still sleeping through the noise. If she's vigorous enough, you might feel even more motivated to wake up yourself when your toddler cries. No one can make you a lighter sleeper, but this should certainly help.

My partner falls asleep putting our daughter to bed, and I feel guilty about waking her up.

My guess is she wants to sleep in a grown-up bed with you, not crammed in with your toddler or slumped in a rocking chair. Besides, as bed partners go, you probably kick less. Don't feel bad about waking her gently and leading her to bed. Her neck and back will thank you for it, even if she's too tired to say anything.

My kid wakes up in the night and wants to nurse. My partner usually gives in. I have a tough time getting back to sleep, and I have to go to work in the morning. Does a twenty-month-old need to nurse at night?

Odds are, at this age, your toddler is nursing because the all-night buffet is open, not because he's hungry. You and your partner need to come to an agreement on how to make night weaning happen. Be prepared to spend a few sleepless nights helping your toddler—and your partner—make this change.

The kindest way to do this is with love, patience, and some toddler-sized discussion. When getting your toddler ready for bed, tell him, "Night-night nursing," so he can get used to the idea that nursing is turned off for the night. When your child wakes up in the middle of the night, your partner should gradually decrease the amount of time she allows nursing. After a few nights of this, she should just go in and briefly reassure or rock your child but not nurse.

Another possibility is for you to take over "nursing" duties for a few nights. When your toddler wakes up, go in to comfort him back to sleep. Since you don't have the same equipment, expect a protest at first. Eventually, though, he will learn that nursing is done during daylight hours. It might be best to deal with this on a weekend, when no one has to get up for work the next day.

My son regularly wakes up at 5 A.M. I want him to sleep to at least 7 A.M. on the weekends. What can we do?
This is a tough one. Early birds are hard to coax back to sleep—it seems to be how they're wired. Much to the dismay of parents everywhere, little kids can't tell the difference between weekday and weekend—it simply doesn't compute for them. The best you can hope for is making the wake-up call a little later every morning. First, make sure you have blackout shades on all the windows in his room, so the sunlight isn't waking him up. Try making naptime a little shorter during the day and pushing back his bedtime so he's going to bed a little bit later. Each adjustment can help a toddler sleep later in the morning. You can also leave some soft books in his crib for him to look at, put a sippy-cup of water by the bed, and keep

your fingers crossed. If it comes down to the wire, you can always bring him into bed with you and try to squeeze in a couple more hours of shut-eye for everyone.

When do toddlers sleep through the night?
When are the Cubs going to win the World Series? The answer is, and no one really wants to hear it, that it's impossible to know for sure. Technically if your kid is sleeping for five hours at a stretch, that can be considered "sleeping through the night." Hardly seems fair, I know, but there it is. Some kids are never, ever going to sleep soundly all night. No amount of thoughtful parenting can change that fact. Some kids go through bad patches when the routine changes. The arrival of a new baby, a vacation, changes in child care, all can disrupt sleep. The important thing is not to get mad at your toddler, yourself, or your partner for your child's sleeping difficulties. Often sleep issues will smooth out by age three. If there were a simple formula, the owner of the patent would be extremely wealthy. Have patience, nap when you can, and remember coffee can be a tired parent's best friend.

On vacation, we changed time zones and had trouble getting our toddler to bed. How do you get your child to sleep on vacation and back to a routine in his own bed when you're back home?
Boy, kids will sure make you pay for that trip to Grandma's or Disney World, won't they? For short trips where you leap over too many time zones, you can simply leave your child on your home time zone. This may mean having dinner at 9 P.M., but it'll save you the trouble of relearning sleep habits when you get home. For longer trips, try gradually adjusting your kid's

hours as vacation approaches. Do the reverse as vacation winds down. Be sure to follow your predictable home routine as much as possible while on the road. Accept the fact that there will be some payback when you return home. It will likely take a couple of days of sticking diligently to your bedtime routine before you can get back down to the business of serious sleep.

We broke down and let our little girl sleep with us while we were traveling. Now that we're home, she still wants to sleep with us.

It's amazing how you can tell a toddler a million times to hold your hand while crossing the street, and she will forget every time. Let her sleep with you just once, though, and it can be harder than heck to get her back in her own bed. Resign yourself to the fact that you're going to have to go through a mini-version of teaching her to sleep by herself again, and it likely will take a couple of days and some tears before things are back to normal. Explain to her that at home, she sleeps in her own bed. Play music for her, get her a special stuffed animal to help her feel secure, and be prepared to put her back to bed several times a night. Be patient—letting her into your bed was your idea.

My daughter can cry and cry for more than thirty minutes when she wakes up at night. The books say not to pick your child up. My daughter cries, my wife cries, and I feel like a rat.

Well, *some* books may say that. Few books push a rigid approach, because every kid is different. Thirty minutes of waiting for someone to answer her cries is a long time in the life of a toddler, and mostly teaches her that you're not available when she needs you. An approach that is easier on everyone is to develop a predictable routine of going in within a few minutes of her awakening, and coaxing her back to sleep with a hug, a little rocking, or sitting on the edge of her bed and cuddling. Make your response predictable, and your toddler will start to respond predictably—by going back to sleep.

CHAPTER 5

A+ Behavior:
The Winning Edge

Biting. Kicking. Screaming. Whining. Yelling, "NO!" No, it's
not John McEnroe losing a line call, or Latrell Sprewell at
training camp. It's just a sampling of the types of misbehavior
you can expect to see from your toddler as he leaves the baby
stage and becomes a full-fledged little person. While your toddler will occasionally push limits and your buttons, your
child doesn't have to be a terror. Believe it or not, it is possible
to handle this phase without spanking, yelling, or threat-
ening.

KNOW YOUR PLAYER

No two kids are alike, even in the same family. Every child is
an individual, with differing abilities and interests, which
means that they're all going to stumble into different strate-

gies to short-circuit your nervous system. So when it comes to the down-and-dirty of discipline, it's hard to plan for every personality. Still, guidelines can come in handy. Arguably, there are two basic toddler types, and once you determine which type your child is, you can create a game plan for dealing with difficult behavior as it comes. Keep in mind that your child may show traits from both types, depending on the situation at the time.

- *The wild child, or physical toddler.* Some kids just have to move. You know the type. They climb furniture, they roughhouse every chance they can. They've colored your walls and, to add insult to injury, the TV. When you call up your neighborhood babysitter, she laughs maniacally before hanging up the phone. If this sounds like your child, give him plenty of activity and exercise to burn off all that great energy. Hit the playground, kick the soccer ball, visit a swimming pool, and bounce around to the Beatles. In short, when in Rome, do as the Romans do. Just try to keep your entire civilization from going down in flames.

- *The shy or clinging child.* Have you suddenly found yourself with a new appendage? You know, the extra weight that attaches itself to your knee as soon as a strange face or situation disturbs his little world? If this is your child, you may need to take a slower approach to things. When your child encounters a new person or place, allow him to express his fears through clinging and words, and gently offer reassurance that "everything is okay." You are the barometer for your child's emotional security, and when you react calmly to the ever-changing world, your child will feel safe.

But expect change. Just when you think you've got him figured out, your kid is going to throw you a curve ball. It's up to you to be prepared to catch it. This means you have to resist the urge to label your kid's personality. If you peg him as shy at two, you may inadvertently reinforce that behavior just by telling the friends and family who drop by, "Oh, don't mind him—he's shy."

Try to describe your toddler's personality traits in a positive way, directing him or her into behavior that you'd like. (Yes, in the end, parenting is all about mind games.) For your shy son, you can say in front of him to friends and family, "He is learning how to make friends." The strong-willed child, on the other hand, is "learning how to do things all by himself!" This provides a natural way to acknowledge when the behavior changes. You can tell your not-so-shy son, "See, you learned how to make friends!"

HAVE A GAME PLAN

Should you use time-outs? Take away the toy when he goes into a meltdown? Whatever you do, make sure you and your partner are on the same wavelength before the situation arises. This will reduce the amount of stress you'll both have when tackling your toddler's behavior. It's important to come to some basic agreements on consequences.

For instance, if you both decide time-outs are the way to go when your toddler's behavior is less than perfect—like the time he flushed your wallet down the toilet—try to remember that your child's attention span is extremely short. If you make the time-out more than a few minutes, he's going to forget what you're punishing him for. (And why did you leave the wallet out in the first place?)

Also, make the consequence fit the misdeed. If your child decides to throw a toy at his playmate, take the toy away. Act immediately. This will help your child see the relationship between his actions and the consequences.

Remember, your toddler doesn't communicate very well yet, so when you tell her not to do something—"WHAT PART OF 'DON'T PUT THE HAMSTER IN THE VCR' DO YOU NOT UNDERSTAND?"—she's likely to hear you without understanding you. Sarcasm will also fly over their heads. Toddlers, especially when they're very young and have just started toddling, don't understand right and wrong. Instead, their behavior is based on simple toddler logic that makes perfect sense from a two-year-old's point of view but may seem crazy from an adult perspective.

WHAT TO DO WHEN . . .
. . . YOUR TODDLER BITES

First, no child *ever* learned to stop biting by being bitten himself. Don't bite him to show him how it hurts. You're teaching him to bite, possibly scaring him, and in the end, it's kind of mean. Besides, your child can't connect his hurt with anyone else's. Biting people is generally an indication of frustration or sensory overload. For toddlers under eighteen months, biting is simply part of how they're exploring the world right now. They don't know how much it hurts: they just know they can do it. Also, teething can cause a toddler to chew on any hard surface that's around. Kids will try to cut teeth on everything from the TV remote to your car keys. Get your child his own set of toy keys to chew on, and he may leave yours intact.

For toddlers over eighteen months, biting can be a method of communication. When biting happens at this age you need to remain calm, comfort the victim if it's the toddler's sibling, and check for injury. Then, as quickly as you can, acting immediately, pick up your little biter and explain, "You can't bite people. Biting hurts!" Recognize the frustration your toddler is feeling by saying, "I know you're (insert the appropriate emotion: mad, frustrated, upset), but biting won't make it better." And then give your child a brief time-out, and you or the biting victim one as well, so everyone can calm down.

Biting should be taken seriously. If you laugh when your child does it, he will think it's a game. It's important to stop this habit before it starts; vampires do not make popular playmates. Talk to your toddler about consequences. For example, "If you bite again we'll go home/be done playing/take a time-out."

. . . YOUR TODDLER HITS, PUSHES, KICKS, OR SHOVES ANOTHER CHILD

Assess the situation—some harmless jockeying around is normal. It's only when the situation gets more aggressive that you need to step in. Separate the kids, comfort and distract the victim, then take your child aside. Explain that hitting (kicking,

ROOKIE DAD TACKLES THE TODDLER

pushing, etc.) hurts and "we don't do it." Keep explanations short and clear. Talk about consequences. "You will have to (have time-out, go home, lose a privilege) if you hit again."

Limit TV, especially violent shows and movies. Children this age are not developmentally capable of knowing the difference between what happens in movies and real life. Kids may just be repeating what they've seen on the screen.

. . . YOUR TODDLER RESISTS TIME-OUTS

Your son refuses to stay in time-out when he's being disciplined. You figure, what's the harm in letting the little bugger go back and play, and your partner wants him to stay.

Here's the quick and dirty thinking on time-outs:

- Time-outs should last about 120 seconds. It's unreasonable to expect an eighteen-month-old to be in a time-out longer than a minute or two. Even when they're two or three, a time-out shouldn't be longer than three to five minutes.

- If necessary, hold your child in place at the time-out, firmly but gently. Compared with your son, you are the size of a gorilla.

- Don't go the other route and make time-out a chance to hug, bond, and talk baseball cards. That makes time-out a reward and encourages tantrums and other negative behavior.

- Time-outs should be held in a quiet, out-of-the-way spot of the home, and during the break, you shouldn't be sitting nearby, watching TV. Your child should know that you're paying attention, and that what is happening is more important than what mess Gilligan has gotten himself into this time.

• The good news is, once you've gone through a few time-out periods, he'll realize you mean business.

... YOUR TODDLER WON'T SHARE OR TAKE TURNS

Younger toddlers can't share or take turns because developmentally they are not ready. Your job is to anticipate the problem—if a friend is coming over, suggest putting the favorite toy or object away. Wherever possible, simplify problems and try to have duplicates.

When you are at the park with your toddler, give her a start at sharing by taking turns on the swing or slide. Let her know what is going on by saying, "Now it's this little boy's turn and then you're next!" "Now it's your turn!" Give your little one positive praise when she first starts taking turns.

... YOUR TODDLER DAWDLES AND DRAWS OUT THE SIMPLEST TASKS

Here is where good planning and having a sense of fun pays off. Avoid morning standoffs by making any task a game. With your biggest grin, say, "I bet you can't get your shoes on before I do." Toddlers love to show off what they know. Ask her for instructions like, "Can you show me how to put your socks on?"

Toddlers get caught in the moment. Try to give yourself (and her) enough time—plan for extra innings. Offer an incentive to complete the task, like "Dad will twirl you around after you are all dressed."

Take time to transition smoothly from playtime to getting ready to go. If she's distracted by a toy or book, tell her she can take it with her, or play with it later.

. . . YOUR TODDLER DRAWS ON THE WALL, THE COFFEE TABLE, THE WINDOWS

Young artists are excited about the power in crayons and markers. Help your budding van Gogh channel that excitement and artistic expression with appropriate equipment. Stick to washable markers and crayons. Keep a supply of paper on hand. Make sure all markers and crayons stay on the table. Tell your artist as she starts to walk away from the table holding a crayon, "Come back, the markers have to stay on the table."

Indulge that desire for a big "canvas" by giving her sidewalk chalk outside. Take the time to draw with her. This is a good time to start showing her letters. For example, draw the first letter of her name. Setting aside some daddy-toddler art time can be a great way to bond with your little artist.

. . . YOUR TODDLER CRIES EVERY TIME MOM OR DAD LEAVES, THE SITTER COMES, OR SHE GOES TO DAY CARE

Separation can be scary and tough to deal with. Your toddler has to learn that when you leave, you will return. Play games to get your child used to the idea of *gone* and *back*. Peekaboo and hide-and-seek prepare a child for the concept of going away and coming back again.

Acknowledge your toddler's feelings by saying, "I know you don't want me to go, but Daddy has to go to work." Be matter-of-fact and go through a regular "leaving" ritual (a kiss, then waving good-bye through the window, for example). Sneaking away doesn't help and can make it worse next time.

Give your son a set of pictures of you and other family members to look at while you are gone. Familiar objects (a toy, blanket, or stuffed animal) can provide comfort.

If you're leaving on a business trip, leave your child with a special object: a key chain, hat, or shirt. This can be your toddler's insurance that you will be coming back.

Be strong. Your child may be upset when you leave him at day care, but don't let yourself be emotionally blackmailed. You know you will be coming back. He will, too. It may not be immediate, but he will understand eventually.

... YOUR TODDLER WON'T PICK UP HER TOYS

It might be time to weed through the toy box if your toddler is feeling intimidated by the task of cleaning up. Don't wait until the mess is huge, with toys strung out everywhere.

Help her break the job down by saying, "Let's pick up the blocks and put them in the bucket." You can make this into a game and join in to make it more fun. If your child still resists, respond by stating, "Then we'll have to take your blocks (for example) and put them into time-out for a day."

Your toddler may not consistently make three-pointers while tossing blocks into the bucket, but cheer her on anyway.

... YOUR TODDLER IS AFRAID OF TAKING A BATH

Your toddler might appreciate water only slightly more than your cat does, so here are some ideas for making tub time fun.

Make the water a comfortable, not-too-hot-not-too-cold temperature. Bubbles are almost a must. Bath books and bath toys can be great treats for toddlers.

Put your feet into the tub with your toddler. There's no better way to coax a water-shy kid into the bath!

Getting shampoo in her eyes can turn the bravest of toddlers off baths. If she is game, let her help wash herself by giving her a sturdy plastic cup to rinse with.

If she pees or poops in the tub, take it in stride. This will happen at least once, if not more! Always have a towel handy for removing your toddler from the tub. Clean up the mess and start all over again. Responding like an angry referee can make your little one fear the tub, so stay cool.

If, after all this, the bath is still out-of-bounds, see if showers are more to your child's taste.

... YOUR TODDLER WON'T GIVE YOU A MOMENT'S PEACE WHILE YOU'RE ON THE PHONE

We've all been there. An important call comes in and your little sport suddenly needs your undivided attention. To distract your toddler, and prevent phone fiascos, put together a box of fun toys only available when Dad or Mom is on the phone.

Give your boy a play phone of his own, available only when you're talking. Or recycle one of your old phones and let him take calls. Your toddler just wants to be like you, so let him play at it!

If you're expecting a call that absolutely cannot be interrupted, make plans with your partner to distract your toddler when the call comes in. If it's just a casual chat, try to make calls after your champ has gone to bed.

. . . YOUR TODDLER WHINES ALL THE TIME

Whining can be his way of getting your attention. He may need a hug, a snack, or even a nap. Sometimes he may get bored and need a new activity, or a change of scenery. Play this one by ear. If you think he has too much pent-up energy, head outside and play.

Whining can grate on everyone's nerves, so remember to set limits. Tell him, "Once is enough. If you keep asking, we won't (insert the proposed activity here)."

Try humor. This can charm your child into obeying, and reminds you to keep his behavior in perspective. For example, say, "Ow! My ears hurt. I can't hear you when you use that voice. Can you ask in your big-boy voice?"

AIM FOR BETTER BEHAVIOR

Here are some tried-and-true approaches that will help reinforce good behavior.

PRAISE GOOD BEHAVIOR

The best way to teach your toddler to behave is to catch him doing something positive—sharing a toy, for instance, or talking nicely instead of yelling—and give him a verbal pat on the back. Toddlers crave approval, and when your child learns what behavior makes you happy, he'll bend over backward to please you.

When you're trying to spot good behavior, be generous. Initially reward behavior that's "in the ballpark." For instance, if your child cleans up at least half of his toys, give him a hug and say, "Good job!" As time goes on, you can expect him to get better and better at behaving—but try not to be a perfectionist.

ELIMINATE POTENTIAL DISASTERS

Toddlers are naturally impulsive, often clumsy, and very "high energy," so avoid situations where they can get into trouble. Put expensive and breakable items up high or in storage. Put your cell phone where your toddler can't reach it, and block off "taboo" areas. Eliminating the temptation can drastically reduce the number of near-misses your toddler will have.

LOOK FOR EXPLANATIONS

Often kids misbehave just because they're kids. Sometimes, however, they're trying to tell you something. If life is tense around your house due to marital stress, or even a round of the flu, your child will pick up on the "bad vibes" and act out accordingly. If so, extra attention and reassurance can solve the problem.

REMAIN CALM

Kids love attention, and often they'll consider bad attention better than no attention. Shy children, conversely, may be so frightened by an angry scene that they withdraw from you.

Give your kid plenty of your attention and handle misbehavior calmly and coolly, rather than blowing your stack.

TRY DISTRACTION OR REDIRECTION

If your child is jumping on the furniture, distract him with another activity. Suggest a walk or a snack, or say, "Hey, look, there's the postman—let's go get the mail!" Toddlers have short attention spans, so the right distraction can change a potential yowl into a big smile.

Channel inappropriate behavior into appropriate play. For instance, if your toddler is banging on your glass-topped coffee table with his shoe, steer him toward his toy workbench and hammer, or give him an oatmeal box and some wooden spoons to use as drumsticks.

PICK YOUR BATTLES

Trust me, you don't want to spend the entire day sending your toddler to time-out. Try to limit the number of rules you establish, and ignore minor infractions. If you set too high a standard for your toddler, he'll be stuck in the time-out corner until he's twenty-five. If his behavior is dangerous, by all means use a time-out to teach him how serious the situation is. If it's just general goofing off, letting it slide may be a more reasonable response.

DON'T BE AFRAID TO SET LIMITS

I know it's tough. Your toddler cries when you turn off the TV, whines when bedtime rolls around, or fusses when you won't give him more cookies. But your toddler needs limits. He'll feel more secure when he knows the boundaries of acceptable behavior and doesn't have to make up his own rules as he goes along. Limits will help him in the future.

TELL YOUR CHILD WHAT YOU EXPECT FROM HIM

It's not fair to expect a child to magically understand vague instructions. Explain to your toddler, as clearly as you can, what you want him to do. For instance, say, "You can put your toys in the living room, but not in Daddy's office." If you're not sure he understands, repeat yourself or offer other clues, such as posting a red Stop sign on your office door. Some children learn best by hearing, while others are more visual, so offer information in different ways and your child will be more likely to figure it out.

SET A GOOD EXAMPLE

Your child looks to you as a role model, so act the way you want her to act. If you model mature behavior, she'll be likely to behave accordingly. You are the First Male in your toddler's eyes, which means that you're the standard she will use to judge men in general, now and in the future.

YOU ARE BIGGER

Sometimes you'll need to use your size and strength to prevent your child from hurting himself or others—for instance, by picking him up and carting him off to his room if he's throwing a fit. Avoid using your size, or threats of force, to frighten your child into obeying. The only lesson you'll teach him is that big people can make little people scared.

The most important point to remember is simply that *you and your toddler are on the same team.* Whatever approach you use, make it clear to your child that you have high expectations because you love him.

Being a toddler is tough—it's like wanting to be a major league baseball player but not knowing what the bases are for.

These new skills come slowly. As your child matures, he'll gain the self-control he needs to rein in his desires, and he'll start responding to your expectations rather than giving in to every urge. This learning process takes years, but it's far more important than simply hollering "No!" every time your toddler acts up.

"Hammerballs"

One to three years

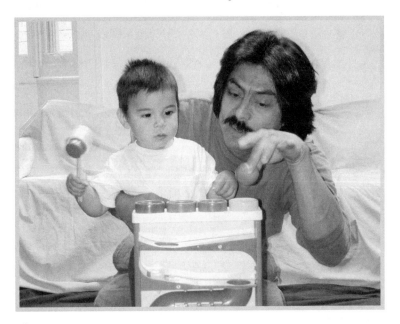

The pounding helps kids handle their anger by learning to hit a ball when they are mad instead of striking another child, and it acts as a tension release. The following activity promotes eye-hand coordination and matching. It also teaches toddlers to wait patiently (hopefully) while it's Dad's turn. This practice in delayed gratification will come in handy later if your child has to share a computer or a car.

• Set up a hammerball game or a workbench with pegs.
• Have him place balls from left to right. This helps prepare him for left-to-right reading.
• Give him the hammer and let him pound the balls.

- Kids over two can practice matching the colored ball to the ring of the holes.

Game tip: *If you're using a hammerball game, set it up before starting this activity. Many active toddlers, especially boys, like throwing the hammerball balls as much as they like pounding them—so don't tempt your would-be pitcher!*

"Animal Box Toss"

One to three years

Win at picking up toys and give your kid some practice cleaning up. Get a head start on the arm strength and accuracy needed for sports. This also helps your child learn and listen, too—we can throw a ball with Dad, but we can't throw our dinner!

- Get together some small stuffed animals.
- For kids ages one to two, stand them near a box, and say, "Where's the dog?" When they find the dog, say, "Woof! You found the dog."
- For kids two to three, practice throwing by standing them a little farther back.
- Count with older toddlers as the animals are tossed.

Game tip: *This game works best with soft toys.*

"Find the Coach"

One to three years

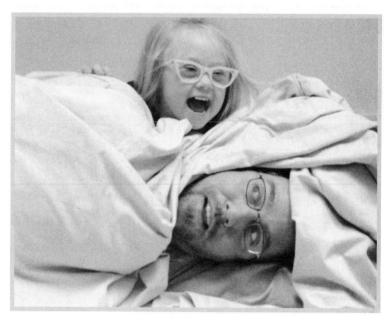

Dad's always there even if you don't see him. "Finding Dad" and other hide-and-seek games help your child tolerate frustration, and they build confidence.

- Hide under a blanket or around a corner.
- Let your child find you, or pop out from behind the corner and surprise her.

Game tip: *Start with a cloth over your face, playing peekaboo with younger children.*

"Follow the Leader"

One to five years

"Follow the Leader" can be a game you play for five minutes in line at the grocery store or when you're waiting in the car for Mom. Every chance your child gets to be in charge, even of a simple game, will develop confidence. Your child also learns self-control, since not very many people can actually be in charge all the time, unless they're the CEO.

• At home with a one- or two-year-old, practice walking on the curb and stopping, offering him a hand for balance as needed.
• In the grocery cart or in the car, you can play games of touching hair, clapping hands, and cheering. Let your child be the leader and imitate his moves.
• Kids will enjoy a simple obstacle course. Show them con-

cepts like *in, out, over, around,* and *under.* Sit down on a pillow, walk around a tree, and jump on the grass.

• Let your child lead the course and even add features.

Game tip: *Follow your child's lead; he'll love being in charge for a change!*

"Tug-of-War"

Eighteen months to three years

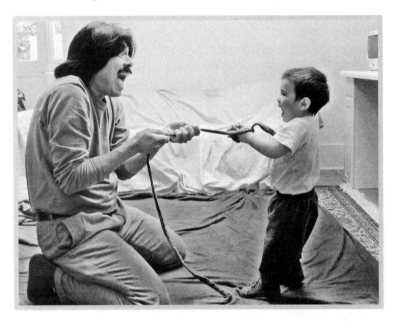

Tug-of-war isn't just for the big guys. True, you can do this with one hand, but your child will feel better if you appear to work as hard at this as he does, with both hands. Your toddler will develop a good, strong grasp, good for that firm hand-shake when he's older. He'll also gain strength in his arms and shoulders, and learn to coordinate his balance when pulling. He'll learn about endurance, follow-through, and why it's so important not to give up.

• Use a rope or ribbon at least three feet long. Let your child hold the rope or ribbon.
• Show your child how to stand with feet apart for balance.
• You pull gently on one end.

- Let your child pull you and lead you around at first, to build his confidence.
- When you pull harder, be careful not to pull him off his feet.
- Build up to stronger tugs with older children so they can build strength.
- Make sure the area for your tug-of-war doesn't have things that would hurt your child if he suddenly lets go.

Game tip: *Make sure you put the ribbon or rope away between games so that it is not accessible.*

"Time-out Chair"

Eighteen months to three years

Sometimes the best way to help a child calm down is to take a break.

- Use two small chairs.
- Ask your child to sit, or, if necessary, take her to the chair.
- You may need to sit next to her to help her stay in the chair.
- Remain in the chair for one to three minutes.

Game tip: *Sit next to or behind her during time-out. To avoid responding to struggling, avoid eye contact with your toddler.*

"Dad in the Dugout"

Two to three years

Learn to think, solve problems, and uncover your favorite spy in training for the FBI.

- Dad says, "I'm going to hide—come find me."
- Dad hides under a table, in the closet, or under the covers in bed.
- Beds and sofas make great fort bases.

Game tip: *This is a great afternoon activity, not a good one right before sleep.*

TIPS FOR WINNING

On long car trips, keep kid-friendly music or stories on CD or tape to play, and try to interact as much as you can (unless you're lucky enough to have a napper on your hands). Use rest stops wisely. Once you let your toddler out of the car seat to run around, he may not want to get back into the car without a long break.

Catch your child being good, and praise him when you see him listening or doing what you asked him to. Watch for op-portunities to say things like, "I liked how you came when I called," or "I like how you picked up your toy when I asked."

Keep things in perspective. If this is hard for you, try concen-trating on your breathing to stay focused. Breathe, and repeat this mantra: *"I am the adult here. I am the adult here. I am the adult here."* Almost everything is fixable or replaceable, except your toddler.

Start every day fresh. Toddler behavior changes from day to day. No matter how out of control your child was yesterday, let him start today with a clean slate.

THE SAFETY ZONE

If you reach the point where you find yourself losing control during one of your child's tantrums, and you actually feel like hitting him, don't stay in the room. Instead, just walk away.

Even the most saintly parent reaches the breaking point once or twice, so don't feel guilty. Remove yourself from the situation until you've simmered down and it's safe to return. This will teach your child that it's better to walk away than strike out in anger—a powerful lesson.

While your toddler needs to learn to follow basic safety rules (don't run in the street, don't play with electrical appliances, etc.), he cannot be expected to follow these rules without supervision. He's simply too young and impulsive to obey even life-or-death rules every time. You are your toddler's best defense against dangerous situations.

Toddlers have no sense of danger. Don't leave a toddler unsupervised or unattended with other children or animals. That friendly neighborhood dog may seem like a safe companion, but toddlers don't know not to grab his ears and pull his tail. Watch for potential dangers, and remember that you are the resident bodyguard.

Hitting and spanking may only make your child more aggressive and angry. Teach your child to use words when he feels frustrated or upset. This can help him learn to express himself safely.

SPECIAL PLAYS

Use an egg timer when roughhousing. This sets a limit before activities get out of hand but still allows the large-muscle, rambunctious activity your toddler may crave. Starting and stopping intense activities helps teach your toddler limits.

Act out behavior problems with puppets. Take turns, letting your child play the parent frequently. When you watch him mimic you in your disciplinary role, you'll be surprised at how he sees you.

If your child is having trouble mastering a new challenge—like sharing toys or cleaning up his messes—give him some colorful stickers, and have him award himself a sticker at the end of each task. A wall chart with toddler-friendly pictures and stickers can be a great motivator!

CALLING FOR THE REFEREE

Deciding how to handle challenging behavior is harder than it sounds. It's important to recognize that you and your partner may have very different ideas on how to handle toddler behavior. Maybe your partner thinks you should nip every potential problem in the bud. Maybe you're happy as long as your kid doesn't burn down the house. Either way, you're going to have different boiling points, and it makes sense to make sure you're on the same page before you find yourself wishing you had purchased more homeowner's insurance.

This means discussing your different discipline strategies. What you can do is arrange to have an evening together when you can take the time to listen to each other, and discuss your strengths and weaknesses openly without judging each other's discipline style. Right. Your last evening together was sometime back in the Clinton administration—or at least it feels that way. Still, do the best you can. Talk to each other in between the commercials on *Letterman,* and before one of you drifts off to sleep. Pick up the conversation when you're driving to your in-laws' and your little one is gazing out the window. The main thing is, try to discuss disciplining before you actually have to do it.

Chances are, even in this enlightened twenty-first-century lifestyle, she's probably spending more time with your child than you are, so if there's some compromising to be done, it's probably going to be more on your end. But that doesn't mean you don't have good ideas, of course, and that's why it's so important to talk everything out with your partner. There are also other benefits, too. The best gift you can give your kid is a good relationship with your partner. Play-Doh probably ranks second.

So, in what cases might you need to start practicing the lost art of compromise? Well, in virtually every case throughout your child's life, you and your spouse will need to be exercising teamwork, from what you both allow your toddler to watch on TV to that toy automatic rifle your uncle gave him for Christmas.

ADVICE FROM THE COACH

My son has major meltdowns whenever we try to go someplace without him—day care, the church nursery, or when we go out for the evening and leave him with a babysitter.

Separating from Dad and Mom is a tough skill for many toddlers. With especially sensitive kids, rehearsals are essential. Have a new sitter come over for a couple of hours just to get to know him while you stand by for support. Spend some time helping out in the nursery so he can grow comfortable with it. When you start a new day care or preschool, visit several times before he starts. Be prepared to stay for quite a while with him for the first few days when he does start.

Congratulate yourself on the fact that your son has such a strong bond with his parents. This will all change when he gets the keys to the car, so appreciate it while it lasts!

My son won't stay quiet during church! It's driving us nuts.
Most toddlers do not have the ability to sit through a sermon and service. That's why so many churches have nurseries. Be sure your son has had a good meal ahead of time and is dressed in comfortable clothes. Try a pew in the back and come equipped with distractions—crayons and paper, small, quiet toys, etc. Try attending just a short portion of the service together, then either you or your partner can leave with your child, letting the other parent conclude the worship service.

My daughter dawdles in the morning when we have to leave for day care. She won't get up from the breakfast table, fusses over getting her hair and teeth brushed, and takes forever to get dressed.
In her own way, your little girl is telling you that she doesn't want to be apart from you for the day. Figure out some incentives and reasonable consequence to get her moving along. The night before, have her pick out her clothes and what she wants for breakfast, and lay the clothes out. Tell her if she finishes her breakfast fast enough, there will be time for a story or short game. If she still won't put on her clothes, cheerfully

tell her, "That's fine. You can go in your pajamas. The other kids will be in their clothes, but I don't mind." If necessary, follow through by putting her clothes in a bag to take with you. She'll figure out that you mean what you say, and she may even beat you to the breakfast table next time!

My daughter touches her private parts and picks her nose. It's embarrassing, especially if she's sitting on my lap, or when we're out in public. Should I scold her?
Scolding is unfair, because your daughter doesn't yet know the difference between "appropriate" and "inappropriate" touching. Simply explain to her, without making a big deal out of it, that people don't touch their private parts in public. (Use a doll to illustrate your little talk.)

My kid grabs stuff, demands toys, and doesn't say thank you
Learning manners is like learning how to hit a free throw—it will take tons of repetition before you see consistency. Every time your toddler demands something, ask that she say "please." Nothing will make you feel like you've turned into your own parents more than demanding to hear *please* and *thank you*, but good manners are essential for helping children develop and be accepted socially.

CHAPTER 6

Healthy Eating Zone: Peak Performance

You might swear more food ends up on the outside of your toddler than inside, and that toast, string cheese, and Goldfish crackers are her only food groups. Welcome to the world of toddler mealtime! Some simple tools can ensure that your kid grows up eating a sound diet.

It's back to basics time; you're setting eating patterns that will last a lifetime. Here are the three big stages you will help your toddler navigate: breast or bottle to cup; liquids to solids; and from being fed to feeding herself.

Your goal is to help all these changes happen easily and naturally while respecting your toddler's desire to do it on her own. You will need some strategy, a lot of floor mopping, and some serious patience.

INTRODUCING THE CUP

For your toddler's first experience with a cup, offer a two-handled sippy cup with a flexible tip. This is a transitional cup and is easier to grab than a bigger cup. When you're first starting out, you might want to offer her the cup after she's had a little snack from the bottle or breast. This will take the edge off her hunger, so she's able to focus more on experimenting with this new object. Choose a colorful cup and let her play with it. This is a whole new experience for her! Make it a game by "practicing" with her—showing her how to hold it and then helping her figure it out. Remember, this may take a while for her to master solo, so be prepared to "practice" a lot.

SERVE IT UP WITH A SPOON

By the time your toddler is around a year old, he's probably started expressing an interest in having his own spoon. Gone are the easy-serve days of just spooning the pureed baby food into his happy mouth. It's time to bite the bullet and let him have his own utensils.

You might want to consider having two spoons at every meal—one for him to experiment with, and one for you to feed him with. He won't get a good handle on spoon-feeding himself for a while yet, so be prepared to wipe food off the floor, table, and yes, even the ceiling. Spoons make great catapults!

Start with food that is easy to scoop, like yogurt or pudding. He'll probably spend some time dipping the spoon in the food, rather than scooping. That's okay. Dipping is good practice, and he'll get the hang of it eventually. Stirring, smearing, dipping, and just general mess-making might seem more fun to your toddler at this point than actual food consumption. It's all part of the game at this stage.

He also might miss his mouth the first ten to fifty times. Let him practice feeding himself and feeding you. He'll learn by doing and by watching you, so be aware of your own table manners, and teach by example.

Tossed salad, anyone?

If your toddler is throwing more food on the floor than in his mouth, he's probably done. Teach him a signal for *done*. For example, when he starts to perform with his food rather than eat it, clap your hands once and say, "Done?" Take the food away, clean him up, and set him free. He will eventually learn how to tell you he is finished by saying "All done" himself.

From around one to two years old, your toddler moves from smooth baby foods to solids, and he starts to use a cup. Trying out new foods can be more about texture and less about taste, so if your toddler wants to take it slowly, let him.

SWITCH IT UP, KEEP IT SIMPLE, AND DON'T FORGET THE DIP

Variety is important. Offer a variety of healthy foods over the course of the day so you know he's getting what he needs; he might not be getting something from each food group at each meal.

To help get your toddler interested in his food, cook simple meals and have him help. For example, roll out pizza dough, spread sauce with a spoon, sprinkle on cheese, and add a face made out of sliced olives. Using cookie cutters, cut shapes out of tortillas with melted cheese on them. Don't forget the dip! Dips are high on the toddler hit parade, and dipping food is a good way for your toddler to increase his hand-eye coordination.

WHEN IS ENOUGH ENOUGH?

When dealing with the toddler appetite, a serving might consist of only a tablespoon or two. So, odds are, when he says he's full, he really is full. With small servings of healthy food you can encourage him to eat well, but don't force him to eat past his sense of fullness.

Also, your toddler's appetite will vary from day to day, so comparing his eating habits with those of other kids his age can be like comparing American and British football—which aren't even played on the same field! Activity level, weather, mood, and just about anything you can think of will affect your toddler's eating habits. This is a good time to just go with the flow. As long as he seems to be developmentally on track, he's probably getting enough.

TREATS ON THE GO AND AT HOME

We live in a fast-food world, but when it comes to your toddler, resist the burgers and fries. Your toddler will have plenty of time to appreciate junk food when she's a teenager. If you skip the fast food now, she'll never miss it.

You might also be tempted to use treats as a reward. Keep in mind that food is energy, not something to be used as currency. So if your little girl starts to get bored in line at the store, don't offer her the nearest candy bar as a bribe to keep her quiet. Granted, you're not made of steel, so let yourself off the hook if you fold once or twice. You should avoid making it a habit, though.

Food preferences created at this stage in the game can stick with your kid her whole life. Modeling healthy eating habits for your toddler will help you both. You'll be healthier for it, and she'll be less likely to have weight issues as she gets older—a win-win situation!

"Dad Aces the Cup Finals"

One year to eighteen months

Stop spills in their tracks. Moving up to the big leagues is easier if you have a cup with two handles.

• Hold your child's hands around the cup.
• Guide the cup to your child's mouth.
• Let your child give it a try.
• It's fun to play with the cup in the bathtub, too.

Game tip: *By age fourteen months, many kids can learn to drink bottled water from a squeeze bottle and begin to practice using a straw. Transition to the cup by offering a cup with a nipple if your child has trouble using a sippy cup.*

"Rookie Refreshment"

Eighteen months to three years

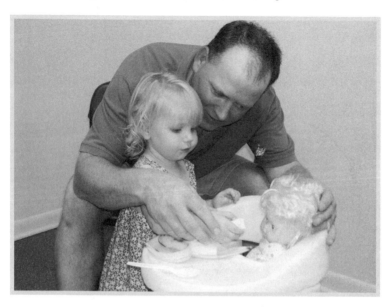

Enjoy a snack together, learn new words, practice taking turns, and get your child closer to feeding herself.

- Place a stuffed animal or doll in a high chair or on the table.
- Encourage your child to give the animal or doll a bite.
- Say, "Yum . . . yum . . . yum!" and let her practice using a spoon or a cup to feed the animal.

Game tip: *Toy stores sell very realistic and inexpensive plastic foods, fruits, and vegetables, which make this activity less messy than using real food.*

"Daddy Snack Attack"

One to three years

Discover colors, get some counting practice in, and learn about temperature with your toddler scientist.

- Start with two popsicles and give one popsicle to your child.
- Have wipes or a wet cloth handy.
- Describe the popsicle, its temperature, and color.
- Find other things that are the same color. "Is your shirt red, too?"

Game tip: *Use a bib and old clothes to minimize mess. If it's warm outside, use a hose or a spray bottle to clean up.*

"Dad Sinks a Three-Pointer"

One to two years

Learning to use a spoon takes some practice. With Dad as coach, watch this skill skyrocket. Practice in gripping the spoon will help teach the fine motor skills needed for all those important activities in life—buttoning buttons, writing, even feeling more confident about making eye contact.

- Have your child sit in a chair or high chair.
- Provide food that easily sticks to the spoon, such as oatmeal, applesauce, pudding, or yogurt.
- Show your child how to scoop up the food with the spoon.
- Then, let him try to feed Dad.

Game tip: *Finger foods such as Cheerios or Kix are great to build fine motor skills and early counting, and they can be fun to sort, as well.*

"The Big Cleanup"

One to three years

Yes, cleanup can be fun! Every meal is followed by another important step—the cleanup. Here is an opportunity to play the name game with different parts of the body.

- Get a warm washcloth or a wipe, and clean up part of your child's face and hands after eating.
- Dad says. "Now I'm washing your nose, cheeks, chin, etc."
- Ask the child, "Where's your nose?"
- Let your child try. You may need to guide his hand at first.
- Let him try to wipe your face, too.

Game tip: *Instead of a quick scrub, pat your child's face clean.*

146

"Water Break"

Two to three years

Squeezing builds hand strength and motor accuracy for handwriting. Bottled water with a squeeze top makes a fun drink and a squirt toy, too.

- Buy small four-to-six-ounce bottles of water with the squeeze, rather than screw-top, lids.
- Enjoy your pint-sized pitcher giving you a drink.
- Drinking water is healthier than sugary juice snacks and prevents tooth decay as well.

Game tip: *Pop these bottles in the fridge for a cold, refreshing drink.*

"Reach for the Goal"

One to three years

Join the toothbrushing challenge. As soon as kids have teeth, it's time to get into the toothbrushing game.

• Kids like to hold a toothbrush, even though most of the brushing needs to be done by parents.
• Sing a song while brushing.
• Practice brushing teeth in the tub. It's fun and often helps kids who resist having their teeth brushed.
• Brush stuffed animals' teeth.

Game tip: *Some children like vibrating toothbrushes.*

TIPS FOR WINNING

Take your toddler with you to the store and have him help name the fruits, vegetables, and other foods you put in the cart. This will make the food seem more familiar when you're sitting down to your meal later, and it might get your toddler interested enough to eat it!

Toddlers can get grumpy if they don't eat about every two hours. Have healthy snacks on hand so you can help keep your toddler's energy level and mood on an even keel. Items like bananas, juice boxes (without added sugar), bottles of water, and cereal are all healthy snacks for when you're on the go.

If you're having a meal out, take some small, quiet toys to keep him occupied while you finish your meal. This is a good time to learn where the family-friendly restaurants in your area are.

Rather than giving your toddler oodles of juice, try diluting it with water by half. Kids love to fill up on juice—it's sweet, easy, and gives instant energy. Unfortunately, it's almost pure sugar and can cut their appetite for healthier food. About four ounces of diluted juice a day is a healthy limit. Also, be sure any juice your toddler consumes is pasteurized.

Offer healthy foods that toddlers love—noodles, ripe fruit cut into little cubes, banana slices, yogurt, ripe melon pieces, dips, crackers, string cheese, and fruit shish kebabs placed on a straw.

Okay, you still might be able to finish a whole pizza in one sitting. Your toddler, on the other hand, might get full after just a couple of pieces of olives and maybe a bite of crust. Serving sizes at this age may be three or four bites. Eating like a bird is normal for toddlers. Just wait, it won't be long before he starts eating you out of house and home.

THE SAFETY ZONE

Carry a travel pack of wipes to clean up restaurant tables, high chair trays, and your toddler's hands when you're out and about. This is also a good time to practice some good hygiene drills by teaching your toddler to wash his hands before every meal.

Even though your toddler may seem pretty self-confident when it comes to solids, choking on food is still a possibility. You'll need to put some foods on the out-of-bounds list for now. Common chokable foods are: hot dogs; peanuts; popcorn; hard beans and seeds of any kind; whole grapes; olives; cherries; corn-off-the-cob; uncooked peas; raw apples, carrots, and other hard vegetables; unripe pears; hard candy; jelly beans; and fish with bones.

Car seats are definite no-food zones—your toddler might choke, and traffic noises make it harder to hear.

Rather than getting to know your nearest emergency room doctor better, cut your toddler's food into small pieces. Try to keep the pieces about a quarter of an inch big. It's a simple step that will save you having to use the Heimlich maneuver.

SPECIAL PLAYS

Play hide-and-seek with a plastic cup by using it to cover pieces of food. Ask your toddler, "Guess what's under the cup!" He'll have fun playing, and he might even eat some of the food you're hiding.

An oldie but a goodie, the "spoon-airplane" game is a good way to get your toddler to eat that one last bite you've been trying to get into him—instead of on him. Of course, you can always substitute his latest transportation obsession. The spoon can become a truck, a bus, or a Harley-Davidson—complete with sound effects.

Get duplicates of your toddler utensils so you can give your toddler his own spoon (or blunt "kiddy" fork), while you use an identical one to feed him. That way you know he's getting at least a little bit of food, and he can practice his skills right along with you. As he gets more practice in, he might even try to "share" his dinner with you.

CALL FOR THE REFEREE

Family mealtimes can be full of expectations, both Mom's and Dad's. Did your family sit down every night for a home-cooked meal? Or perhaps your idea of a family dinner involves standing up in the kitchen, eating buffet-style? No matter what childhood memories you bring to mealtime, you and your partner will need to come to terms with what you want for your own family. Maybe you can even discuss it over dinner!

Your kid can't seem to sit still for an instant at the dinner table. You want to make your daughter stay at the table until everyone is done, but your partner wants to let her go. With a situation like this, it's important to face a few facts. Toddlers have the attention span of a puppy and shouldn't be expected to sit at the table for more than ten to fifteen minutes. It is especially true for the youngest toddlers. Trying to force your toddler to stay at the table when she is very obviously done is only going to make for a stressful meal. Relax a little, realizing that in time, she'll make it through an entire dinner. You might even want to consider feeding your toddler first, so she can go play while you eat.

Your kid wants dessert, but he didn't finish his dinner. Your partner says yes, you want to say no. Who's right? Memories of being stuck at the dinner table to finish that one last piece of asparagus might pop up at a time like this. Here's where you need to remember that food is just that—food. Treating dessert as a reward will only give your toddler the message that sweets are treats and are *way* more exciting than the meat and potatoes on his plate. Go with your partner on this one. Your toddler won't start to see dessert as the goal line, which will save you some huge mealtime battles in the long run.

• • •

You like health food, and your partner wants to let your daughter have Froot Loops. It's time for some food negotiation. First off, realize that your partner is half the equation. You can't dictate exactly what she's going to do as a parent, but you can try to compromise. Try sitting down to explain your concerns, and work out some reasonable ground rules for feeding your little one. While you may see Froot Loops as the end of the world, your partner may have grown up on them—and she turned out all right, didn't she? Aim for a healthy diet, but keep the lines of communication open, and accept that your daughter will, at some point, be exposed to food that you find less than wholesome.

ADVICE FROM THE COACH

My kid drinks from bottles but really doesn't want to eat solids.
He's like a pitcher on a winning streak. Why mess with the pregame ritual and screw up a sure thing? The truth is, some kids have strong reactions to texture. You might want to start with really runny food and encourage him to have fun with it. If he just had a bottle, wait a while before bringing on the solids so he'll be a little bit hungry when you offer him food. Try not to rush him. Be sure he sees you enjoying your food— you can even make a show of how delicious it is with some "mmm" noises and lip smacking for effect. He wants to copy you, so help him do it by providing little bites for him when you're eating. Above all, relax. If you're stressed about what he's eating, he'll sense that, which will only make this phase more frustrating for both of you.

My son seems so underweight, and his arms are so skinny. He just doesn't seem to eat much. He takes two bites and that's a meal. I am concerned he's not eating enough calories to grow.

After the round cheeks and chubby fingers of babyhood, it can be kind of a shock when your kid slims down. However, it's very normal for kids this age to be thin. They're tremendously active, working on their motor skills, and it's almost like they're designed at this age to be more aerodynamic. If you are still concerned, check with your son's doctor. Most likely, he's just fine and falls within normal weight percentiles or ranges. Once the doctor gives him the all clear, relax—the muscles will come later.

My child will only sit in the high chair for five minutes to eat, and then she's done. I would like to have a nice, leisurely meal.

Ah, the distant dream of every parent of a toddler—a nice, quiet, leisurely meal. Unfortunately, your toddler just isn't designed with that in mind. At this age, meals are more like mid-flight refueling and should be short and frequent. If you still have dreams of a nice family meal, try having breakfast together. Breakfast is a better meal for family togetherness, as your little princess is rested, ready, and full of energy in the morning hours. As for dinner, someday the day will come when your girl can make it all the way through to dessert. This isn't that time, though.

I am concerned that my child is overweight. She can scarf a whole sandwich down in one sitting, and she polishes off bags of chips like there's a potato shortage going on.

First off, check with your toddler's pediatrician. Is she within normal weight percentiles or ranges? This is also a good time to do a reality check on your family's pantry. Do you have shelves stuffed with chips and cookies? Are fruits and vegetables available in kid-friendly sizes and shapes and offered regularly? Are you offering reasonably small portions? Most important, is junk food just an occasional treat, or is it a daily staple? If your daughter feels the need to inhale her snack, make sure it's something that's healthy. Also, make exercise a part of your daily routine. These steps will help your child create healthy habits for life.

Taking our toddler out to a restaurant has become a real challenge. She doesn't want to sit in the high chair, and she wants to play with the salt and pepper shakers—and everything else within reach. Food always ends up on the table and floor, and it looks like a disaster area when we get up to leave. Help!

Restaurants are challenging for toddlers. First, try to stick to family-friendly restaurants. Once you are there, clear a spot on the table so your toddler can only reach the things you want her to reach—like her food and toys. Bring crayons, a couple of books, or a quiet toy, and take turns eating while one partner takes her for a stroll. This is definitely not the time to take your little angel out to a four-course meal. Expect dinner to be brief, and save the truly fancy restaurant meals for nights when you've managed to snag a babysitter.

My child makes a huge mess when eating and doesn't know how to use a spoon. My partner feeds him because it's easier, faster, and a lot less messy.

Hey, wouldn't it be great to just sit back and have someone else spoon your food into your mouth for you? Taking over the messy end of mealtimes is a tempting trap for parents to fall into. However, it isn't in your child's best interest. The mess can be daunting, but he needs to learn how to handle his own food intake, and putting the ball in his court is the only way to do it. Besides, by handling the spoon more often he'll soon get the hang of feeding himself. You'll probably be surprised at how quickly he improves. If the mess is too much for you or your partner, try stripping your toddler's clothes off before you let him at it. Put a splat mat under his chair, or try feeding him outside if the weather is cooperative. Offer foods that create less mess, like toast, small pieces of ripe fruit, or small pieces of cheese.

Is there any way to have a pleasant meal with a toddler in attendance? I love my boy, but I'm craving some adult conversation over the dinner table.

It's important to make some time for "grown-up" talk, and mealtime is one consistent time you get to spend with your partner. Of course, now that you have your toddler there, the conversation is probably geared more toward "Open wide for the airplane!" That can wear on even the most patient adult after the millionth time. Try having your meal with your partner after your boy is in bed, or get a babysitter to watch him while you go out for some adult conversation and food.

CHAPTER 7

Scouting for Talent: Covering All the Bases

Do you have visions of your toddler growing up to be a home-run hitter, an expert golfer, a marathon runner, or even the next Wayne Gretzky? If so, now's the time to introduce him to the fitness habit. Athletes aren't born the day they step onto the ice. It takes years to develop eye-hand coordination, timing, motor skills, muscle tone, and strength, and as your toddler's first coach, you can start training him now.

WHY SHOULD KIDS LEARN SPORTS?

If you can teach a boy to throw a football or dribble a basketball, you can teach a girl the same skills. And don't worry about your little girl being too delicate for macho sports; if you think females are fragile, check out a WNBA game, or watch Venus and Serena Williams smash hundred-mile-an-hour serves over the net. The days when girls were believed to be wusses are long gone!

Of course, not every kid is interested in sports. One mistake some dads make is to pressure kids to take up the sports that they themselves excelled in—"I know you can throw a fastball, kid, it's in the genes!" Many kids are writers or artists or musicians at heart. So introduce your toddler to sport and exercise, but if he's not as enthusiastic as you about kicking a soccer ball or tossing a football, you'll find plenty of other non-athletic activities to enjoy together. Even if your kid is more Mozart than McEnroe, however, teach him the importance of keeping his body healthy and fit—because that's a lesson that will help him live a longer, better life.

FOLLOW THEIR TALENTS SO EVERYONE WINS

What if you're an athletically challenged couch potato—the last guy chosen for basketball, the perennial junior varsity third-stringer, the bookworm who doesn't know a double axel from a double fault? It doesn't matter. And it doesn't matter, either, whether your toddler grows up to win Olympic gold or simply learns to have fun shooting horseshoes in the backyard and playing flag football with his friends. It doesn't even matter if he's all thumbs and has two left feet. What's important is teaching your child that physical activity is fun, and that fitness pays off.

WORKOUTS MAKE EVERYBODY FEEL *GOOD*

A child who loves to throw footballs, run races, jump hurdles, climb hills, and swim laps is likely to become a healthy adult. He'll also be less stressed out, because he'll have a healthy outlet for his tension. In addition, he'll be less likely to develop love handles and a beer gut; research shows, not surprisingly, that children who spend time playing sports or working out stay leaner than those who spend their days glued to the Nintendo exercising only their thumbs. "Daily physical activity for children needs to become a priority for parents equal to that of buckling seat belts," says child health expert James Hill, Ph.D. "Lack of physical activity is a major reason why children's obesity levels are at all-time highs."[1]

In addition to keeping your toddler in good shape physically, sports help build life skills that he'll need both on and off the field. When your child succeeds at a sport, he'll grow more confident. When he loses, it'll teach him a valuable lesson in coping when things don't go his way. He'll learn perseverance, problem-solving skills, and sportsmanship, and he'll learn that practice and hard work can lead to big wins—a lesson that will pay off in the classroom and the workplace later on in life.

Moreover, the physical skills your toddler will master through sports and exercise will improve his school performance. By swinging a bat, hitting a croquet ball through a

---

[1] Hill is quoted in "Physical activity message for parents from new survey: No more excuses," press release of the International Life Sciences Institute, Washington, D.C., July 1997.

wicket, tossing a basketball through a hoop, or knocking a golf ball into a hole, he'll learn concepts about spatial relationships (over, under, in, out, through, around, etc.). And sports will improve his motor planning skills—his brain's ability to organize and carry out a sequence of unfamiliar actions—which will help him in the future when he's learning a new computer program, drawing a picture in art class, or practicing a musical instrument. In addition, when your child practices a sports skill over and over, he'll be improving his attention span and building a sense of comfort with repetition that will help him perform school tasks requiring focus and practice.

MAKE A DATE TO STAY IN SHAPE

Need still another reason to get off the couch and take up family sports? A kid who exercises or plays sports regularly is less likely to drive you nuts, partly because he'll burn off excess energy, and partly because exercise causes the body to crank out "feel-good" chemicals called endorphins, which can put a child in a better mood. A half hour of toddler sports each day can translate into fewer temper tantrums, tears, and time-outs, as well as less "hyper" behavior. Sports and exercise wear kids out, too, so an active toddler is likely to put up less of a fight when it's time to go to bed.

Of course, a one-, two-, or three-year-old isn't ready for tackle football or tennis. What your toddler *can* do is learn the sports basics, from how to catch and kick different sizes of balls, to how to swing a miniature bat. He can play at swinging a badminton racket, throwing Nerf darts, or picking up a ball with a Velcro mitt, even if he's much too young to play a real game. He can also imitate your golf swing using a child-sized plastic club, or make his first strike using a scaled-down set of pins and bowling balls. He won't be very coordinated at any of these activities, but he'll be learning the basic skills he'll need later as an athlete.

More important, he can learn how to use his body, the ultimate sports tool. Of course, your child's build and genes will play a big role in determining which sports he'll master. (Shaquille O'Neal wasn't cut out to be a cross-country runner, and Michael Jordan proved that he isn't a natural-born outfielder.) But almost any physically fit child, tall or short, large or small, can excel at one sport or another. So teach your child how to use his body. Encourage him to exercise alongside you when you're working out. Show him how to do sit-ups and jumping jacks. Practice exercises that improve his fine-motor and hand-eye coordination, such as beanbag tosses, block stacking, Nerf basketball, hopping, jumping on both feet, or standing on one leg. Most of all, let him know how exercise makes his body stronger, faster, and healthier. And show him that *you* exercise regularly, because kids love to copy their dads.

If it's possible, establish a fitness routine with your child. For instance, schedule a workout with your toddler each Saturday morning, followed by a "Daddy-and-me" breakfast. As any exerciser knows, the hardest part of working out is getting in the habit, and it's easier if that habit is ingrained early on. By combining one or two regular exercise sessions a week with daily sports or other physical activities, you'll be setting your toddler on the path to a healthy life. Moreover, with your mini-personal trainer around to nag you until you get out of bed and start moving, you'll probably find yourself getting more "buff," as well!

Most of the time, your child will be delighted to join you in any games or exercises. To a toddler, even crunches look like fun the first few times. He'll also enjoy simple games and activities such as playing catch, kicking a ball back and forth with you, swinging in the park, paddling in the pool, running an obstacle course, shooting baskets, and throwing rocks in a pond. Help him learn eye-hand coordination by blowing bubbles while he chases them and pops them with his index finger. Put an inflatable "bopper" in his room, and teach him to give it a few whacks when he's feeling frustrated. When you take him out in his stroller, alternate riding with walking. With a little imagination, everyday activities can become part of your toddler's fitness routine.

"Balance in the Basket"

One to three years

Take your first mate for a ride in an imaginary boat. She'll have fun pretending to be a sailor, and she'll pick up some skills needed for soccer or football: balance and muscle strength.

- Place your child in a laundry basket or cardboard box. The box should be big enough for her to sit in comfortably but small enough so she can comfortably grab the sides. Put a pillow or blankets inside to keep her snug.
- Move the box from side to side, making motorboat noises.
- Or put the box on the floor and push it around the house.
- Say, "Whoa, there's a big wave," or "Look—a fish jumped."

Game tip: *Practice playing catch with stuffed animals or a ball of newspaper while your child is in the basket.*

"Toddler Rebound"

One to three years

Shooting hoops with your toddler will build arm strength and timing. He may even make a basket or two! Hold the backboard at child's shoulder level for this game.

Game tip: *These inexpensive plastic backboards work best with a soft Nerf ball.*

"The Catcher Rules"

One to three years

Kids need good hand-eye coordination for everything from sports to writing. Help him gain a leg up with a game of catch.

- Get a Velcro catcher's mitt and ball set.
- Show your child how to put the mitt on.
- Holding the ball, put your hand next to your child's hand.
- Slowly toss the ball, aiming directly at the mitt at first.
- Slowly move your hand farther back while tossing the ball.

Game tip: *Help your child learn how to grasp the ball by asking him to put the ball on Dad's head and arms.*

"Toddler Toss Up"

One to three years

Every kid likes to fly high with Dad. Flying through the air increases your child's coordination and also helps your child's back become straight and strong.

• Hold your child around the waist and lift her up.
• Say, "Now we're going up, up, up!"
• Encourage the child to say, "Up, up, up!"

Game tip: *Playing this game over a bed or a carpeted floor is safest.*

"Kick Ball"

One to three years

Set your toddler on the road to soccer stardom. Here is a great play to practice equilibrium, timing, and concentration.

- For a toddler under two, provide support: either stand behind the child or stand him against the wall.
- Place the ball against his foot.
- Encourage him to kick the ball.
- Gradually place the ball farther away from his foot.
- For a toddler two or over, set up cones or boxes, and help him kick the ball around the cones or into a wastebasket.

Game tip: *Take the ball to the park and practice kicking it. For indoor practice, kick a balloon.*

"Tour de Toddler"

Fifteen months to three years

Do you have fond memories of a childhood spent on the seat of a bike?

- You'll need a kid's bike that fits your child. A bike with a narrow seat is best. Her feet should easily touch the ground.
- Find a site with a slight incline for a head start.
- Place your child in a sitting position on the bike. Push her around slowly, until she's comfortable.
- Teach her to push the pedals with one foot, then another. Most kids push backward at first.
- Once she's mastered pedaling, encourage as needed.

Game tip: *Using a helmet makes for a safe ride.*

"Slide into Home"

Fifteen months to three years

Burn off some extra energy and teach your child about heights and safety. Everybody needs good balance, and it's easiest to learn when you're having fun. Sliding also shows how to be safe with stairs.

- For kids fifteen months to two, help them up the slide, and catch them at the bottom.
- For safety's sake, keep tabs on kids ages two to three.
- Encourage your child to go down backward when he is first using the slide.

Game tip: *Excellent slides can be bought for thirty to fifty dollars. They're a great investment, keeping kids from climbing the walls when you can't get to the park or the weather's bad.*

"Shooting Hoops"

All ages

This activity builds arm strength and improves motor accuracy for the day he gets his driver's license.

• Put the hoop on the floor. Encourage your toddler to put the ball in the hoop.
• Hold the hoop while your child drops the ball in.
• Practiced pint-sized hoopsters can throw the ball into the hoop.
• Dad says, "You made the shot! Good job! Two points!"

Game tip: *Soft Nerf-type balls are best to begin with.*

"Golf Pro"

Eighteen months to three years

The next Tiger Woods may be watching *Sesame Street* in your living room. Try this with him. You'll reap dividends that include getting ready for handwriting and handling two-step directions. Your little pro might be building the skills to go to college on a golf scholarship!

- Get a toddler golf set.
- Show him how to hold the club.
- Then practice hitting the golf balls. Don't expect a birdie out of him until much later!

Game tip: *Putt the ball into a cardboard box for indoor fun.*

"Swim Meet"

All ages

Kids just can't get enough pool play. Want your child to start learning those crucial water safety skills, start building up those muscles, and learn to love working out with Dad? There's no better place than a swimming pool. While in the water, kids gain coordination for later sports skills and get a head start for those future swim classes.

- Water is a lot more fun and less scary when Dad is close.
- Take it slow and easy.
- Water toys, including fish that float and plastic magnetic fishing poles, distract kids from being fearful.
- Twirl around with your child, playing airplane.
- Bathing suits with inserted floating panels can make the water more fun for your child.

Game tip: *Kids will swallow water. Make sure to keep their heads above water. Swim diapers prevent accidents in the pool.*

TIPS FOR WINNING

Hell hath no fury like a toddler whose TV gets turned off in mid-cartoon. However, you'll do your toddler a favor by limiting his television time, because research shows that a child is nearly five times as likely to be overweight if he watches more than five hours of TV per day.

The best kid sports games are the simplest ones that require little or no equipment. For instance, ask your toddler to show you how many times she can jump up and down, how long she can walk on her tiptoes, how far she can jump (measure her distance so she can try to beat her record), how far she can throw a ball, or how far she can carry a paper cup half-filled with water without spilling it.

Avoid pressuring your toddler to be interested in a sport that isn't his cup of tea. Expose your toddler to a variety of sports equipment, from pint-sized golf clubs to soft baseballs and basketballs, and follow his lead, rather than feeling disappointed if he doesn't follow in your athletic footsteps.

When you're teaching a new sports skill, break it down into small steps; for instance, work on catching a ball first, then on bouncing and catching it, and later on dribbling.

Start out simple. When you play catch, start about one foot away from your toddler and gradually work up to two and then three feet. When you play basketball, begin with a really big "basket," such as an office trashcan, and practice from only a foot or so away.

Enjoy the experience of playing sports with your toddler without worrying about how many times he catches or drops the ball, or how successful he is at making a basket. It's the process, not the outcome, that counts at this stage.

Toddlers have an attention span of about five to ten minutes (when you're lucky), so plan short sports sessions and quit when your child has had enough—even if you still want to play.

SAFETY ZONE

Toddlers can hurt themselves seriously if they're not supervised around exercycles, Stairmasters, weight benches, and similar equipment. If you own exercise equipment, keep it safely locked away when you're not using it. And tell your toddler it's off limits, because he's too small for adult-sized weights, bikes, and exercise machines.

Keep your toddler's exercise area free of sharp-edged furniture and other potential hazards, and work out with her on a carpeted or padded floor.

When your toddler gets revved up, it can be hard for him to stop. Be sure his environment is safe—for instance, that he isn't too close to the street if he's playing outdoors, or to breakables if he's indoors, in case he can't "put the brakes on" in time.

As your toddler gets taller and more agile, keep "kid-proofing" higher and higher. Figure out how high she can reach, and remove anything dangerous within a foot of that level.

Gate stairs in your own home, and bring a portable gate if you are visiting friends or relatives with stairs—unless you want to spend the whole time standing between your child and the stairway.

SPECIAL PLAYS

Does your toddler like races? Challenge him with creative variations. For instance, do a "change of pace race," in which participants run to one side of the yard and then crawl back on hands and knees. Or create a "hat race," in which participants must change hats at the end of each lap.

Set up an obstacle course, and then do your best Howard Cosell imitation as your child goes through the course: "She's coming around the corner now . . . yes, folks, she's cleared the cardboard box, and she's heading for the pillow climb . . . take a look at that form . . . and we have a winner!" She'll love the extra attention and beg to play again.

Place a two-by-four or a row of large blocks on a well-carpeted surface, and let your toddler use it as a balance beam. If you use a board, be sure it has no rough or splintery edges.

Play the hokey-pokey game and ring-around-the-rosy. Sure, it's corny—but your toddler will enjoy it, and you'll both get a great workout.

CALL FOR THE REFEREE

Your partner is content to let your little boy toddle around the park for exercise, but you want him to start learning about more organized sports. You've bought him a pint-sized backboard and his first T-ball set—now the fun of raising a son begins, you think. But she says you're pushing him too hard. Well, both of you are obviously coming from different places. Your partner may have grown up without any experience in organized sports, while you have fond memories of Little League. Reassure Mom that you have no intention of timing your little boy, or keeping score, and make your sports time together fun and low pressure. He'll love the attention from Dad, and bit by bit, he'll develop the skills he needs to develop a lifelong love of fitness.

Your partner loves skiing, and Picabo Street is her hero. She's already bought your two-year-old little princess her first pair of skis and plans on hitting the kiddie slopes with her later this year. You've got visions of frostbite and broken legs and aren't sure if your girl is ready for skiing. Don't worry so much. It's likely that your bundled-up toddler will love some time in the snow. Ten to twenty minutes is about the maximum amount of time kids will listen and follow directions for ski instruction. After that it's time for simple snow play, then off to the lodge to warm up. Little kids get cold very fast, and it's vital that grown-ups keep close watch on the fingers and toes.

You're worried about water safety and want your toddler to start swimming lessons. But Mom thinks she's too little and says she should be four years old before starting. Toddlers really can't learn to swim until they're over four—your partner is right about that. But parent-toddler swim classes are a lot of fun for everyone, and it gives your little one some good exercise. Your child won't be water-safe for years to come, though.

You see no harm in letting Junior scale the stairs, although your partner is in danger of going into cardiac arrest. Letting your toddler explore can be a terrifying experience, especially when you realize your son has no fear and sees stairs as an adventure waiting to happen.

Toddlers love stairs. They would go up and down all day long, given half the chance. Stair climbing is the type of skill where you *don't* want them to learn from their mistakes. Be one step below them at all times, until the climbing and coming down have been mastered—which may not be for months.

Navigating the descent will probably take your toddler a lot more time than learning to climb up. You'll need to get down next to your toddler and show him how to go backward down the stairs—feet first on his hands and knees. This is the least dangerous move for a beginner. And don't start practicing at the top of the stairs; start going down together just a few steps from the bottom. Because if you do it from the top and there is an error—well, your imagination can figure out the rest.

Especially in the beginning, make sure your partner recognizes that you are aware of every move your toddler makes. Unless you're a complete klutz, this will reassure her and reduce the hand-wringing.

ADVICE FROM THE COACH

My daughter is fearless on playgrounds. Last week she climbed to the top of the slide and tried to jump off. Luckily I was there to stop her, but she nearly gave me a heart attack. Why doesn't she understand she could have broken her neck?

Because toddlers (much like teenagers) fully believe that nothing serious can really happen to them. Also, toddlers don't yet understand the laws of the universe. While you can instinctively see that your daughter will get clobbered if she walks in front of a moving swing, or that she'll be injured if she falls from the top of the slide, her grasp of physics is nonexistent.

In time, as your daughter gets scrapes and bumps and other "ouchies," she'll gradually begin to understand that your warnings make sense. In the meantime, stay close and protect her from herself!

My partner and I like to take short walks as part of our fitness plan, but our toddler gets bored quickly if we take him along. Is there any way to keep him interested, so he doesn't start whining after we've gone ten steps?

Turn your walks into treasure hunts. Before you set out, give your toddler a paper bag and tell him he'll be looking for four or five different items. (Write them down, so you can mark them off as he finds each one.) Your list might include a leaf, a stone, a flower, a dandelion, a pine cone, or an interesting weed. Or play a variation of the car game I Spy by telling your child to keep an eye out for several special objects—a truck, an apple tree, a dog, etc.—while he's walking. (To make this more fun, put small cars, toy dogs, etc., in a paper bag, and have him pull out the toys one at a time and look for the real-life objects they represent; for instance, if he pulls out the toy dog, have him search for a real dog as you're walking.) Also, pack a little bag of snacks to keep him occupied.

How far can you realistically expect a toddler to walk before getting tired? Probably about two blocks, so take a stroller along if you're planning to go farther.

I get home late at night, so outdoor sports are usually out of the question except on weekends. What's a good indoor game that will give us both some exercise?

Try a safari. Tell your daughter to stay in one room with Mom while you hide an assortment of stuffed animals out in "the wild." Then follow your daughter as she searches for the animals: offer plenty of clues. (For instance, hide a stuffed bear under a bed, and tell her, "This animal is hiding in a cave—we'll have to crawl on our tummies to find it!") Put some animals up high, on piles of pillows, so she'll have to climb to reach them; place others inside cabinets, on beds or chairs, inside closets, or even in the tub. Keep some rooms dark, and use flashlights to uncover your quarry.

Here's another animal-theme game that provides lots of exercise in a limited space: pretend to be rabbits hopping, snakes slithering, bugs crawling, kangaroos jumping, or elephants swinging their trunks. Take turns choosing which animal to imitate, and add lots of sound effects. You'll be working on pretend play, taking turns, and physical fitness all at once. (You may also discover that your toddler has an unexpected streak of creativity. One suggestion I've heard a toddler toss out: "Be a baboon butt.")

I've already spent a fortune on my own fitness equipment. How much stuff do I really need to buy for my toddler?
Not a lot. Balls of different sizes are important, and push toys, pull toys, and riding toys will exercise different muscle groups. Nerf bats and basketball hoops are excellent toys, but you can make your child a basketball "net" using a box or wastepaper basket, and your toddler can use a wrapping-paper tube to bat very soft balls. Stuff it with paper to make it sturdier. Slides and climbing toys are great fun, but if you can't afford them, just visit the nearest playground.

My son doesn't seem interested in sports or any other kind of exercise. After about five minutes, he wants to quit. Is he going to be a total couch potato?
Grown-ups tend to think of exercising as a half-hour or hour-long activity, and we're accustomed to spending hours playing sports games. To a toddler, however, five or ten minutes is a long, long time. Concentrate on very short games (for instance, a quick round of "trashcan basketball," or a race around the yard) rather than forcing your son to play for longer periods. As he matures, he'll be ready for ten- or fifteen-minute exercise sessions.

My three-year-old seems real clumsy. We've been playing baseball with a kid-sized bat and ball for months now, but he still can't hit the ball. I was a varsity baseball player in college, and it's frustrating to watch him fail. What can I do?

In the first place, relax! By the time you'd reached college, you'd been playing baseball for nearly two decades. Your son's total experience probably adds up to ten or twenty hours. And hitting a baseball—even a kid-sized one—is a very difficult skill that takes lots and lots of practice. Your son will improve with time.

Also, think back on your own childhood. Did your dad, your brothers or sisters, or your friends have talents you didn't have? And were you talented at sports they couldn't master? Of course, because we aren't carbon copies of each other. Your son may yet grow up to be a great baseball player—or he may be a dud at baseball and a star at soccer, tennis, or swimming. It doesn't matter, as long as he learns to enjoy sports and fitness.

CHAPTER 8

The Big Celebration: Bye Bye Diapers

You've cleaned up more blowouts than you can count. The time has finally come for potty training, this is Super Bowl Sunday! No more dragging the diaper bag everywhere—you can almost smell the freedom.

This is an exciting time for you and your toddler. It's your chance to be the Trainer of the Year. Potty training is a challenge for everyone involved, but there are plenty of tricks to help make it run as smoothly as possible.

READY, SET . . . GO?

Is your little pitcher ready for the big leagues? Your first job is to decide when to start. You need to assess your little player's strengths and look for signs that he is ready for this step.

As far as physical readiness goes, your toddler's bladder

and bowel muscles aren't mature enough to handle toilet training until he's at least two years old. Added to that is the difficulty of explaining the physical process of pooping and peeing to a toddler.

When he does start pretending to use the toilet, ditching his diaper when it's wet or poopy, examining his "equipment," or telling you when he needs to be changed, he's probably ready to start learning about the whole potty experience.

Some kids are about as interested in potty training as they are in brussels sprouts. If your toddler hasn't asked about or shown any interest in using the toilet by age three, it might be time to get on the potty and begin. Sometimes you have to gently push past "no." A strong-willed kid is likely going to take more time and patience than a more relaxed one.

DIFFERENT GAME PLANS

With boys, peeing is the bigger challenge. First, decide if you're going to start him off sitting or standing. If you go straight for standing, teaching him to aim will be your top priority. Floating targets—like bits of toilet paper or Cheerios—can help him practice hitting the water rather than the floor and walls. Show him how it's done—he'll want to do it "just like Dad."

When it comes to pooping, you'll need to show him the ropes again. Your toddler wants to be like you, so let him see you using the bathroom to help him understand what he needs to be doing. This includes teaching him how to wipe. Having a handy stash of pre-moistened, flushable wipes is helpful when your toddler is learning how to wipe.

Girls have it a little easier. Everything happens when they're sitting down. Teaching them to wipe from front to back is especially important with girls, as they are more susceptible to urinary tract infections.

With both daughters and sons, praise every little step they make toward being potty trained. Impatience and criticism will only serve to make this process seem longer for both of you.

Why does Daddy have a . . .

At this age, kids really tune into the differences between boys and girls. Don't be surprised by frank questions. Toddlers are like teenage boys—they're very interested in their own body parts—and other people's, too.

Avoid getting mad at your kid for exploring his or her genitals, but do mention that it's something people do in private. Girls may be very interested in why men have penises, and why boys get to pee standing up. Your daughter might even want to watch you pee. Curiosity is normal at this age, so explain or show as far as you're comfortable and then move on.

Also, be prepared for children to want to touch their pee or poop. They're just checking out what they've produced. Explain what it is, and then use the opportunity to teach some thorough hand washing.

SLOW-PITCH OR FASTBALL?

There are a couple of different approaches you can take toward potty training. One is a methodical, slow approach; the other tries to get it done in one weekend. They both require lots of patience. If you go for the weekend method, you should probably tackle it during the warmer months.

Take a weekend and start it off by stripping your kid from the waist down. Without diapers, she'll actually see what's happening when she pees or poops. She probably won't like having pee running down her leg, so the concept of peeing in the potty becomes more attractive. This method is best pursued in the great outdoors, since it can be hazardous to carpets and furniture.

Changing diapers in midstream

Some parents who otherwise use disposable diapers swear by switching to cloth diapers during potty training. Disposable diapers still feel comfortable when wet or poopy, unlike cloth diapers. Kids in cloth diapers tend to potty train faster than those in disposables. You can expect some protests if you try this on a toddler used to disposables.

The slower approach starts with familiarizing your kid with the potty, and the idea of going potty. Have him sit on the potty with his clothes on, so he can see how it feels. Let him explore the potty chair, and tell him what the parts are for.

The next time you visit the potty, have him sit on it with a bare bottom. Talk about what happens when you use the toilet. Watch him for signs that he needs to poop or pee. If the opportunity strikes, have him use the potty—but only if he's willing.

Encourage your kid to use the potty after a meal and when he's first up in the morning. If you have more than one bathroom in your house, let your kid pick out his main pit stop. Dress your child in that bathroom in the morning, using the time between changing diapers and getting dressed as a chance for him to sit on the potty. Make it part of your morning and evening routine: take pajamas or clothes off, use the potty, wash hands, and get dressed.

Make sure he's wearing clothes he can remove on his own. Pants with an elastic waist are helpful at this stage. Avoid moving him into underwear until he's successful on the potty about 70 percent of the time. Expect to have to help him undress to use the potty for a while. Wiping carefully is not something your toddler will master right away, so be prepared to help.

Your toddler probably won't be ready to go solo for quite a while. The whole potty training process (including getting through the night dry) can take anywhere from three months to a year—though rarely longer. Be positive about the process, and your toddler will be, too!

Accidents will happen—they're as inevitable as Lance Armstrong winning the Tour de France. Don't make a big deal of it when your kid doesn't make it to the potty. Be matter-of-fact during cleanup, and lavish your child with positive attention when he does manage to make it to the potty on time. The more attention you pay to the successes, the more likely they are to happen.

STAYING DRY AT NIGHT

Kids often master being dry all day before they can stay dry at night. To help decrease nighttime wetting, limit liquids after 7 P.M.; have your child use the potty right before bed; consider getting him up to use the potty later, like when you go to bed; and have him use the potty first thing in the morning.

Staying dry at night probably won't happen until several weeks—or months—after you've conquered the daytime training. Most kids are night-trained around age three. Sometimes this can be tougher for boys, but don't despair! Use a waterproof mattress pad under a fitted sheet in your child's bed or crib, have a good supply of clean sheets in store, and be patient.

"Team Potty"

Two to three years

*G*et ready to retire from diapers: Tap into your child's wish to "be a big kid."

- Give your child one of your special baseball hats.
- Let him wear it only when he's sitting on the potty.
- Pretend you are doing a sports-type commentary. Say things such as, "Now (your child's name) is sitting on the potty!" "I'm so proud of him." "Something might come out soon!"
- Read a story to pass the time.
- Do a potty cheer.
- Call Grandma to make the big announcement.

Game tip: *Sing "Bye Bye" potty song before flushing.*

"Dolly's Game to Try"

Two to three years

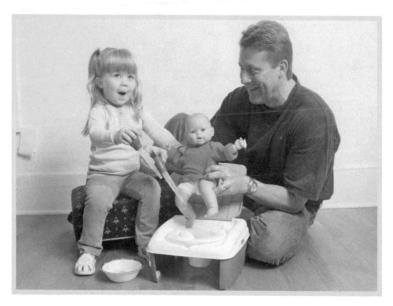

Here's another way to help your child learn all about the potty in a fun and painless way. It will really help "connect the dots" on what the potty's all about.

• Put a doll or stuffed animal over a child-sized potty.
• Give your child a squirt toy.
• Help your child aim carefully and cheer for your child when the water goes into the potty.
• Say, "Soon you will be going potty all by yourself, too!"

Game tip: *Kids like dolls that match their "parts," so look for an anatomically correct one.*

"Take a Good Shot"

Twenty-two months to three years

Want your kid to feel on top of the potty training process? Here's a way to get her involved.

• Fill a baster, eye dropper, or squirt toy.
• Hold a container and ask her to squirt the water into it.
• For kids over two, encourage your child to squirt water into the potty.
• Plastic cups are also fun to fill up in the bathtub.

Game tip: *Squirt or spray bottles are fun outside toys in the backyard to water plants or trees.*

"Aiming for the Hoop"

Two to three years

Learning exactly what the potty is for isn't easy. Here's a game that will make the bathroom a fun place and get across an important idea.

- Go shopping with your child and purchase two plastic squirting toys.
- Position your child in front of the potty, and show him how to squirt water into the potty.
- Take turns squirting water into the potty.

Game tip: *Remove rugs and mats from around the toilet and plan to do a quick mop-up after practice.*

"Postgame Wrap-up"

All ages

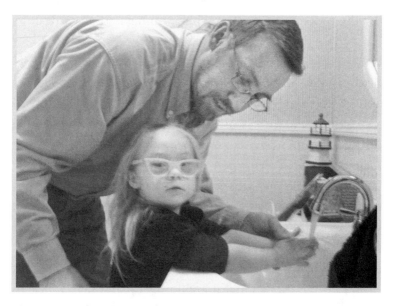

Pass the soap and water and clean up together after using the bathroom. This will help nail the final step in the process, teach your child how to do things in order, and get an early start keeping hands clean.

- After using the potty, have your child step up to the sink.
- Squirt some soap and demonstrate how to wash up.
- Turn on the water and check water temperature.
- Provide help as needed to wash hands.
- Let your child turn off the water with help from Dad.
- Offer help drying and end with a high five.

Game tip: *A stool will allow your child to be at a comfortable height to use the sink, and it will promote independence.*

TIPS FOR WINNING

Wait until both you and your partner are psyched about starting the process. Try to start when you have some extra time, like a three-day weekend.

Be prepared! Bring a change of dry clothes, including shoes and socks, wherever you go. Also, carry plastic bags with you so you have a place to store wet or soiled clothes when you're out and about.

Get some books and videos on potty training at your local library. Share them with your potty-training rookie so he can see other kids using the potty.

Pick words everyone is comfortable with for bodily functions. Keep in mind that your child will pipe up and say, "I have to go . . ." at the most awkward moments, so the words you choose are important.

To avoid having your child dread potty time, keep potty sitting to under five minutes. Potty training isn't a race, and the more you push, the longer it might take.

Dress for success. You can make the process a lot easier by dressing your kid in clothes that are easy to pull up and down. Spring and summer, when it's warmer, are often good times to start, because kids wear fewer and lighter clothes then.

In the beginning, use pull-ups or training pants when you're going out, for an extra margin of safety. This will let kids feel the wetness but spare the car seat. Wait to tackle underwear until your kid can stay dry about 70 percent of the time.

Avoid making negative comments about smells or body parts. The aim is to teach your child how her body works, not to make her feel bad about it. Praise goes a long way in making this process go smoothly and quickly.

Have a potty party to celebrate the first success. Decorate the bathroom with streamers. This is a big step toward independence for your toddler, so make a big deal out of it!

Let your kid pick out special underwear as an incentive to making it to the potty more than half the time—otherwise you'll be doing a lot of extra laundry. Whether they're sparkly Dora or Thomas the Tank Engine underwear, the more your kid likes them, the more she'll want to use the potty instead of wearing diapers.

SAFETY ZONE

Keep the bathroom door open and supervise the potty process. Kids shouldn't be left alone in the bathroom. Most kids are capable of emptying the soap dispenser and unrolling full rolls of toilet paper in less than thirty seconds.

When kids hit the potty training stage, it's time to stop changing them on the changing table and start changing them on the floor. Toddlers love to jump off anything and everything—and will, if the opportunity strikes.

Have your toddler wash his hands every time he uses the potty. Make it a habit. Be consistent and it will just become part of the process.

SPECIAL PLAYS

Bring a doll or teddy bear and have it use the potty when your child is using one, too. If you can, find an anatomically correct doll to teach your child about her body. Let the doll "use" the potty, and show how everything works. This can help speed the learning process.

For a boy, throw a few Cheerios into the potty and tell your little squirt to try to hit them. Demonstrate how it's done.

Keep a stash of special toys in the bathroom, only for use after a successful potty time. Of course, measure the success in terms of small skills—like pulling her own pants down for the first time, or remembering to get the pee *in* the toilet.

Have a special song you only sing in the bathroom. Take a favorite tune and rewrite the lyrics to fit potty time. Getting to hear the special song when they are successful can be a real incentive to toddlers.

Let your kid wear your special baseball hat when going potty. You might end up having to wash it if it goes for a swim, but it will give your child something special to look forward to when he's learning how to use the "grown-up" toilet.

CALL FOR
THE REFEREE

Potty training can be stressful, for both kids and parents. You can see that the end of diapering is near, and you might get impatient for your child to jump this hurdle into the big-kid world. Discuss with your partner how you want to approach this task, and have a plan for the weeks ahead. Be patient! This will all be over soon enough, and before you know it, your kid will insist on wearing the same pair of ratty SpongeBob Square-Pants underwear every day for a month— just like the big league guys do when they're on a winning streak.

Sometimes you think your kid has "accidents" on purpose. Your partner thinks your daughter is trying as hard as possible to potty train. The whole thing is just frustrating to you. In these cases, parents need to have a meeting of the minds. Find a compromise between pushing for independence and providing emotional support to your little one. You might be expecting too much, too soon, and Mom might need to push a bit more. Have patience with your daughter and your partner. You all have the same goal. Don't make a big deal out of accidents, or kids may become fearful of using the potty.

Your kid won't go on the potty and doesn't seem interested in potty training right now. Mom wants to ease up, but you want to keep trying. Take a short break. Frequently toddlers will decide they are ready to participate in potty training. It can sometimes take months for a child to learn how to use the potty.

You think Mom is the best one to handle the potty training; your partner wants your full-on participation. Nobody wants to scrape poop off a three-year-old's bottom and out of his underwear, but you've both got to take turns doing it. That way your child knows that potty training is important to everyone and is a family project. Step up to the plate—you need to be an active participant in this process.

ADVICE FROM THE COACH

My kid doesn't want to sit on the potty. She won't even pull her pants down!
Let your kid sit on the potty with her diaper and pants on—you gotta start somewhere. It's incentive time! Try a signing bonus: the promise of a twirl or an airplane ride, or reading a favorite story only if she's sat on the potty. Let her play with a cool toy in the bathroom if she's sitting on the potty. Casually make sure she sees you using the toilet; kids want to be like their parents, and she might catch on quicker if she knows you use it, too. Encourage her to use the potty before or after her bath, when she's already undressed.

My kid won't go in public restrooms!
Frankly, some grown-ups don't like them either—they're

noisy, sometimes smelly, and full of strangers. Try finding the biggest stalls possible in the quietest possible restrooms. You might want to consider getting a folding, portable toilet seat for your toddler—they can make the public potty seem less scary. Another option is to bring a potty chair along on car trips, lined with a plastic bag.

My kid insists on taking off all of her clothes when she uses the potty, not just pulling down her pants. This makes it into a HUGE ordeal—and it's so unnecessary.

Take comfort in the fact that your girl is taking it seriously and wants to do a good job. Talk to her about it before she needs to go. Have her watch Mom in the bathroom, with Mom explaining it all step by step (probably for the millionth time). Watching other kids use the potty at preschool or day care can also help—enlist the teacher's assistance with the issue. This phase will pass when she's more used to the process.

My kid will use the potty if I put him on it, but he'll never tell me he needs to go or use it without prompting!

Hey, it's a process, and a real complicated one with lots of skills, and it takes time to figure out each step. You'll need to hone your observational skills and watch for signs that he's ready to go. Then, try making it into a game. Offer to race him to the potty. Once there, show him how to pull his pants down. Then, when he's nailed that, tell him to use the potty. Stand at the door and talk him through it. You may need to put him on the seat at first. When he's done, tell him to wipe and wash. Again, you'll probably need to help at first. Gradually cut back on the amount of assistance you give. Try offering him a prize for telling you he needs to go—like some one-on-one time with Dad. And realize that just *going* in the potty is huge for toddlers—figuring out when to go will come in time. One day, he'll simply go in and use the potty all by himself and then be mystified why everyone is acting like he won at Daytona.

My kid sits on the potty but won't go. When I take him off, he instantly pees on the floor.
He's learning control, just like you did when you figured out how to throw a curve ball. Mostly, he simply doesn't understand that pee and poop come out of his body. Sometimes just standing up can trigger the urge to pee. Patience is the key. Have a towel ready for accidents, and be prepared to promptly sit him back down. Avoid getting angry—it'll just make him afraid of the potty.

My kid was interested in potty training and was potty trained before she was two. Now she's going backward and only wants to wear diapers. Help!
This can be a problem with kids potty trained too early. If you need to go back to diapers for a while, do it. Relax—the harder you push, the harder she'll fight you. Remind her that she's a big girl now, and when she goes back to big-girl underwear and using the potty, there are big-girl bonuses—like a trip to the zoo. This is a time when bribery won't get you thrown out of the game. Big changes in a little person's life can move the process backward, too—a new baby in the house, a new sitter or day care, starting preschool, or moving. Time will help, along with gentle encouragement.

CHAPTER 9

Dad of a Boy: His Hero

You finally got what you always wanted: a son. You'll throw the baseball to each other in the backyard, you'll give him pointers on how to ask a girl out on a date, and you'll laugh at the Three Stooges and wonder why your wife, and all of womanhood, doesn't seem to appreciate them. You'll teach him to shave, how to drive, and now you have somebody to mow the lawn.

Some of the good stuff—okay, most of the good stuff—you're still waiting for. After all, this is a toddler we're talking about, and you're recognizing that a lot of what's going on isn't in your comfort zone. He cries over the silliest things. He wants to give you wet, sloppy kisses, and you're thinking, "Well, you know, guys don't do that . . ."

You're starting to realize that you may have a son, but you still don't know what the heck you're doing. And you almost passed out the other day when your wife had the guts to say,

"You know, our son might not want to play shortstop for the Chicago Cubs. He might want to do something else for a living, like become a musician or a teacher."

Because as horrified as you are, you know she's right. . . .

DAD'S THE MVP

Mostly, you want your son to grow up to be somebody you can be proud of, someone who could conceivably be the president of the United States, someone who will be rich enough to support you in your old age. Failing that, you're at least hoping your son doesn't grow up to rob a 7-Eleven as part of his career plan. Well, if you have dreams for your boy, you can't just phone in parenting. As the saying goes, it may take a village to raise a child, but all you need is a village idiot to ruin everything. You need to really *be* there for your son. Not to get all sappy about it, but your little boy needs you.

And it isn't easy. There's no formula that will guarantee your success as a dad. If you want him to grow up to be brave but not a bully, a nice guy but not a ninety-eight-pound weakling who gets the tar kicked out of him every time he is outside, you're going to have to work at this parenting thing, where you're either present or on call twenty-four hours a day, seven days a week. That's just how it is.

Unless you're an at-home dad, obviously a lot of times you aren't there. And the sheer amount of time a mom spends giving care to kids, from feeding to baths, can create a tight bond that will sometimes make a father feel that there's no room for him. But you need to wedge yourself in there. Hopefully you did that from the moment your son was born. Hopefully, from the get-go, you were helping to feed him with breast milk in a bottle, playing with the little guy, etc. But if you didn't spend much time with your son then, thinking, "Well, I'll bond with the little guy later," guess what? It's later. If you haven't been giving your son quality time, start doing it now! It will be the most rewarding—and fun—work you'll ever do. To grow up strong and confident, boys need regular time with Dad. Your little boy, as young as he is, needs to be with you and wants to be with you.

When you're the dad of a toddler boy, you want him to grow up to be the sort of man people can turn to in a crisis, a regular combination of John Wayne and James Bond. But you start envisioning showing him those movies, and suddenly you have an image of your toddler giving another preschooler a judo chop at the playground. You want him to be a smart, strong, successful, all-around good guy—not somebody who's going to have a bull's-eye on his back for the neighborhood bully. And for dads who had distant dads who were around but never available, trying to imagine how to be a good father can seem next to impossible. After all, if you don't have much of a role model to look up to, how do you know if you're actually being a good father? If there are things you enjoyed doing with your dad, your son will probably enjoy them too.

PLAYING A GOOD GAME

You can do no wrong in your son's eyes. Seriously. Studies show that most little boys idolize their dads, and most of us instinctively know that that's the case. Boys think their dads can do anything, and they want to be like their fathers. That means as long as you're doing your best, you really can't go wrong, especially at this age. Take your son to Home Depot: You might think you're just running a small errand, buying a crescent wrench or whatever, but to your pal, it's a fun house of colors and shapes and possibilities. You can show him what you know, and he'll soak in a lot more than you think. And if you look at some gadgetry and have no clue what it is, your son isn't going to care. If he's one or two years old, telling him, "That's a tool" is just fine. He isn't going to demand that you track down a shop clerk and ask exactly what it is.

Obviously, much of parenting is the same whether you've got a boy or a girl. You help your child to learn important things, like looking both ways when crossing the street, how to use the potty instead of diapers, and how to eat at a table in a way that doesn't resemble a scene out of *Animal House*.

But boys are definitely a different animal to parent from girls. Boys face life with a go, go, go attitude: they climb, they run at full tilt, they jump off anything and everything. They love to shove stuff in holes, so you've got to police the house so they don't jam a fork in an outlet or stuff a tuna sandwich in the VCR. They often need less quiet time or downtime than girls do. They'll literally run until they drop, which, if you don't stop them, will probably be late at night. They need a dad's help in channeling that energy in fun, useful ways. In other words, they need somebody they love, but are a bit intimidated by, to rein in their excess energy and keep them focused.

So wrestle with your boy. Swing him around in the yard (carefully, of course). Teach him to shake hands. Hug and tickle him. (Sure, in print, it looks wimpy, but c'mon, guys, this is the twenty-first century. You're allowed to hug now.) Give him piggyback rides. You can be a one-man amusement park to your son.

YOUR LITTLE CHAMPION

Young boys are often more aggressive than girls (though not always). If they get mad, they might shove, push, or hit until they get their own way. Like the manager of a young Golden Gloves prospect, your job is to get your boy to learn control in a way that helps him to be a winner.

If your son looks like he's about to clobber a playmate, as quickly as you can, kneel down to his level so you're eye to eye. If time is totally of the essence, put your arms around him, or pick him up to restrain him. Then tell him, in the simplest possible language, "We don't hit." You don't need to go into long-winded detail about why it's bad to pound on a playmate—he doesn't care. Most of that will simply go over his head when he's so worked up.

NO UNNECESSARY ROUGHNESS

For many dads, it can be really tempting to swat your son's bottom after you've just seen him slug a friend or family member. Don't give in. It will just teach him that big people have the power to hurt little people, and that the use of force will resolve hot situations—not a lesson you want him to learn, and not a lesson that will teach him how to behave better the next time he gets into it with a friend. (Yes, maybe your father, and even your mother, spanked you. No, you didn't turn into an ogre or rob a bank. You even return your library books on time. But think about it. You're teaching your son to not hit by, uh, hitting him?)

If your boy doesn't look like he's going to calm down anytime soon, separate the kids, take a time-out, leave the playground, or sit with him in a car until he's cooled off and can play again. Boys have short fuses when they are angry, and Dad can help his little buddy pull himself together with a little contact and coaching.

HIS MOM, YOUR WIFE

The Cubs vs. the Braves. You and your son? Yeah, some fathers feel competitive with their sons the moment they arrive in the delivery room. If you haven't felt that, great. If you have, well, you understand. Your boy was all your wife thought about during the pregnancy, and after. And granted, we're talking breastfeeding, but sometimes you may feel that your son's getting more action than you are.

This is how it's worked for thousands and thousands of years. Your feelings are natural and understandable, but in the end, you need to be supportive of your son's need to spend time with his mother, and you just have to be the grown-up. It's not as if you can't spend time with your wife, or be intimate with her. You just need to strategize with her a little more so you're both working on getting quality time with each other.

Surely there's somebody who can babysit your little

buddy. Your parents, your in-laws, your neighbors' kid? Maybe somebody at your office has a teenage daughter who babysits, or maybe you know somebody at church. Even if funds are tight, hopefully every once in a while, you can grab a sitter just so you and your spouse can try to remember what attracted you to each other in the first place. Or every Friday or Saturday evening, maybe you'll decide to have "date night" inside your home, where you two pull out some candles and pop something in the VCR, and see if anything leads to anything. If you talk about ways to spend more time with each other, somebody's going to come up with a solid plan.

If you tell your partner in a nice way that you're kind of jealous of your son because he's spending so much time with her, chances are you'll both come up with a solution, and your spouse is likely to be quite impressed that you care enough to bring this up. If you're like a lot of guys, chances are you've just been waiting for things to get back to the way they used to be, and your partner has been wondering if you care that all of the romance in your marriage seems to be deflating like an old tire. So take action now!

"Making the Cut"

One to three years

Your new recruit hasn't had a haircut before, and it isn't something he's looking forward to. Before the big day, have a mini-barber session at home.

- Grab some stuffed animals or action-man figures.
- Let your child practice giving them a pretend haircut. Make a V shape with your fingers and say, "Snip, snip, snip!"
- Let your child pretend to snip Dad's hair or give the stuffed animals a haircut.
- On the big haircut day, accompany your little player for his first haircut and take a picture.

Game tip: *If your little fella is uncomfortable with the barber, have him sit in your lap while his hair is cut.*

"A Close Shave"

Sixteen months to three years

Help your son get a taste of being a grown-up man while catering to his desire to shave.

- Get a popsicle stick or tongue depressor.
- Put some shaving cream on your face, and let him "shave" you with the stick.
- For age two and over, you can put some shaving cream on your son's face and let him try to shave himself with the stick.

Game tip: This activity is best for kids who have stopped putting everything in their mouths.

"Firefighter Hero"

One to three years

Check out some real-life heroes and their gear during a weekend day or holiday. Meet a fire engine up close and personal.

- Let your child touch the fire truck.
- Point out colors and letters on the truck.
- Explore the hoses and ladders.
- Shake hands and take pictures of the firefighters and their trucks.

Game tip: *Firefighter plastic men are great toys to bring with you, and they'll help your son remember the visit to the firehouse.*

"All Aboard Daddy"

One to three years

A win-win situation: give your child the opportunity to build his balance skills and connect with Dad.

• Squat down and help your child onto your back.
• Have him clasp your shoulders.
• Give him a tour of your house, yard, or park, while securely holding on to his legs as they wrap around your waist.

Game tip: *If your toddler is still drooling, wear old clothes.*

"In the Locker Room"

One to three years

Soap up and have fun with Dad! Play ball and go fishing for plastic toys in the tub.

• Run a bath of warm water.
• Take a bath together or clean the tub together with a spray bottle.
• Pour water in and out of containers.
• Squeeze water from a sponge ball into a funnel and watch the water drain through.
• Stick plastic letters, numbers, and shapes to the side of the tub.

Game tip: *The tub is a great place to practice pouring or squirting.*

"Team Building"

Sixteen months to three years

There's nothing a boy likes better than being with "the man," his dad. And what's better to visit than a construction site?

- Hold your child as you watch the construction. Imitate the sounds of the machinery, the hammering, or the trucks.
- Teach him the names of the equipment.

Game tip: *Plastic tools in a kid-sized toolbox "just like Dad's" are a real hit with your little builder/mechanic.*

"Check Out the Pros"

Two to three years

Check out Dad's baseball cards or even a deck of playing cards. Holding the cards builds fine motor skills.

• Point out different players, colors, and shapes.
• Encourage your child to find a specific color or shape by saying, "Where's the player wearing the red shirt?"
• Practice counting cards together.

Game tip: *Dealing out the cards can help kids learn to take turns.*

"Dad and His Little Squirt"

One to three years

It's a heap of fun to take aim and hit a tree with Dad! Here's a way to develop separate finger movement for motor accuracy and handwriting skills.

- Fill up a plastic water toy.
- Encourage your child to look at the target.
- Place the child's hands over the trigger.
- Say, "Ready, set, go!"
- Encourage your child to take aim and hit.

Game tip: *Toddlers love to squirt water on the sidewalk and make designs.*

TIPS FOR WINNING

Remember that hug Mark McGwire gave his son when he set the record for most home runs in a season? So make like McGwire and hug him. Not just once, or on special occasions, like doing well in a sport or on Thanksgiving. Parenting's a contact sport. Hug your son every single day, until he goes off to college, if he'll let you.

Every day, take the time to say something positive to your son. Try to be specific—like "That's a really cool garage you're making out of the box. I like how that dinosaur is stomping on it. Wow, cool idea."

Go out together every weekend without Mom. A trip to the grocery store or hardware store alone with Dad is fun, and it will give your partner some much-needed alone time and a break.

When you play games let your boy win on occasion, whether it's racing to the car or shooting basketballs at a kid-sized hoop. It'll do wonders for his ego.

How you treat your spouse is often how your son will treat *his* own wife when he grows up. So—and hopefully you've been doing this all along—treat her with respect and affection.

Offer choices: "Should we go to the slides first, or feed the ducks?" Or "Would you like crackers or a banana?" It's all about giving your little son a sense of power and turning him into somebody who may grow up to be a leader, rather than somebody who always follows.

SAFETY ZONE

Don't insult your kid. It can be hard not to, when he's done something frustrating like spilling a gallon of milk—all over your checkbook. But insults, even seemingly harmless teasing, often backfires with little kids, who don't understand kidding or sarcasm. They think literally.

Okay, you're human. One day, despite your best intentions, your temper boiled over faster than an old Buick's radiator on a hot mountain pass. If you yelled at your son, apologize. He won't think you're the weaker for it, and because he loves you so much, he'll forgive you, probably in nanoseconds. You're also teaching him to say he's sorry when he messes up when he's older—like when he'll invariably back into a police car when you're teaching him to drive. Trust me, you'll be very glad he's learned to say "I'm sorry."

Watch him carefully at the park, because a toddler boy can't—or won't—pay attention to his limits. Actually, no self-respecting toddler pays attention to his or her limits. Falls from slides, swings, and the jungle gym all can lead to big-time injuries. So stay close by, and if he's scared about climbing a ladder or some other activity, don't push him. He'll come to it in good time, and a little caution is better than having to ride with him in an ambulance to the emergency room, in addition to years of guilt because you urged him to tackle something he clearly wasn't ready for.

Belt that little Houdini in, whether it be in a car seat, a stroller, a high chair, or a shopping cart, to keep him from falling. Putting a car seat on a shopping cart, incidentally, is one of those surprising but common ways to accidentally injure your child. Lots of people do it, but one cart bumping into yours can send that car seat tumbling off the cart. Serious head injuries or other problems from such falls land toddlers in the hospital *all the time.*

Toddlers overheat easily. Never leave a kid alone in a car, even if it doesn't feel that warm out. Let's repeat this: NEVER LEAVE A KID ALONE IN A CAR. This includes running out to pick up the mail, paying for gas inside the store, or dashing into a convenience store for a quick coffee or soda. Cars heat up *much* faster than you think. And even if you lock your car, you are leaving your child exposed to any creep who walks by and thinks, "Hmmm, a kid, and he's alone." The newspapers are filled with stories every summer of children who were left in cars, only to die in under half an hour. The rest of the year, there are enough stories of kidnapped infants and toddlers from cars. *Just don't risk it.* And incidentally, on the subject of toddlers overheating, carry a stash of bottled water in cars and strollers, and offer it frequently.

As he gets a little older, your little boy might fight holding your hand in parking lots or crossing the street. Don't give in. Even when they can talk really well, little kids are lousy at judging traffic.

It seems like a great father-son bonding thing to watch wrestling or boxing together. But think again. It can really scare your kid, or lead to aggression. And if he gets the bright idea to try out those TV moves on a playmate, he could inflict some real hurt on a friend.

SPECIAL PLAYS

There are some times in toddlerhood that almost demand a dad's presence. One of the most important is when a boy gets his first real haircut, so be there.

Car washes are always cool for little kids, especially the do-it-yourself ones. Let him help you soap the car, or give him a rag to rub the hubcaps. Break down the task into small bites so he can understand it.

Have a secret handshake, or come up with something that just you guys share. The older he gets, the more elaborate it can be. Start with a variation on a high five, throw in a pat on the back, and work from there.

CALL FOR THE REFEREE

There are going to be times when you feel like you and your wife simply aren't the young, cool couple you imagined you would be. Your son is always in your wife's lap. You're covered in everything from snot to oatmeal, or whatever your son has on him.

Keep in mind that this is natural, and eventually you and your partner will find your groove. And what they all say about kids growing up so fast is true: eventually you're going to miss these days.

Sometimes your son is going to be the victim of a playground bully. You're going to be mad, but if you can't keep your temper, you're going to teach your son to constantly lose his. He needs to learn self-control as well as self-protection.

Someday you're going to buy a gift for your son that your partner will hate. It's inevitable. Maybe you've bought a toy gun. Your partner doesn't want him to play with it; you can't see what's the big deal. You played with toy guns, and your face isn't on Wanted posters across the country. Compromising is probably the answer. Your partner may have a point that a toy automatic rifle isn't something your twenty-two-month-old is ready for. But a light saber might be a different story.

ADVICE FROM THE COACH

My son pushes my wife around, and it really ticks me off. She sometimes has to tell him to do something five or six times before he does it.

Oh, the selective hearing of a toddler. He's not alone, believe me. Before you land on your kid hard, talk to your wife and tell her that twice, max, is all that any parent should ask. For instance, if he won't come to mealtime when asked the second time, go get him by the hand and lead him to the table. If he was playing with toys when he ignored you, put those toys in a time-out for a day. His listening will get better over time if you are consistent. Also, bear in mind that boys often listen better to Dad, so you've got a natural advantage over Mom. A boy wants his dad's approval more than his mom's.

It really bugs me when my son acts scared for silly reasons, like when he sees clowns at the circus or other kids in Halloween costumes. Even the mascot at baseball games can scare him.

Well, it's hard to blame a little kid for thinking that circus clowns can be kind of creepy. After all, they're strangers and look like nobody he's ever seen. A dad telling him not to be afraid isn't going to help. A couple of things may help. Stay away from clowns and circuses until he understands it's just makeup. Second, several weeks before the next Halloween, buy or check out some children's books on the holiday and read them together. Help him plan his own costume, like wearing a small Lone Ranger mask over his eyes. And skip the trick-or-treating for now—a party for the little kids at your local library, mall, or community center will probably be a lot more to his taste than walking through a dark neighborhood with lots of teenagers dressed as ax murderers. He's barely out of babyhood, after all.

My son just bawls when my wife goes out. What's the deal? What can I do so he wants to spend time with me?

Toddlers—boys or girls—want to be with whomever they spend the most time with. In most families, that's Mom. It's that simple. But you can help coach him through it by planning a fun activity when Mom's about to leave. Get out the DustBuster and vacuum the car, or have a favorite book handy. Be free with the hugs. Do some special guys-only games that Mom doesn't do—like pretending to be a twirling rocket ship. With many children, the storm's over fast; any tears dry before she's backed out of the driveway. In other cases, it's like getting to the Super Bowl: it takes practice, practice, practice before your son doesn't cry when Mom goes. But he'll get the hang of it with your help.

Sometimes my son will actually tell me to go away—that he just wants to be with Mommy.
Don't take it personally—though it's tough not to! This happens often when a toddler is tired, sick, or feeling clingy because of some change in his life, like a new teacher at day care or a fight with another kid. He also just plain likes that soft Mommy bod, just as you do. So grin and bear it, and realize that real soon, Mom's going to be the one feeling a little left out when you two troop off for an afternoon of Little League together. Dads are strong and exciting to little boys, and he'll figure it out.

I don't like my wife to be naked in front of our little boy. He stares at her!
Every family's got a different level of comfort with nudity. You've obviously reached yours. Talk to your wife and tell her you believe it's time she puts on a robe before she leaves the bathroom. But don't make a big deal out of it with your boy—he'll sense you're weirded out about it, and that will confuse him.

My son asks why his mommy doesn't have a penis and if she lost hers.

Kids, like racehorse handicappers, always look for what deviates from the norm. Your son also wants to be just like you. At this age, the simpler the explanation, the better. Tell him that boys have a penis, girls don't, and each model is just fine. Pretty soon he'll be on to other topics, like why the cat doesn't want to be shampooed.

My kid has the attention span of a gnat. I really want him to help me on chores like washing the car. But he stops after a moment and starts playing with the hose. It really pushes my buttons!
You wouldn't expect someone from the junior varsity bench to instantly outplay the starting seniors, would you? You're just expecting too much. A couple of minutes is exactly the attention span of the average toddler. You'll only get yourself worked up for nothing if you expect something he can't deliver. And it's not fair to him, either. Over time, his attention span will get longer. Remember, he's a kid, not a Marine recruit. He's got all the time in the world, so let him be a child.

My son doesn't want my help with his train set. He got mad when I rerouted it after I brought home a new drawbridge for the Thomas the Tank Engine set.
Would you like it if your boss completely redid your project without asking? Your son might have put a lot of effort into putting the track together the way he wanted it. Say sorry, and remember, it's not what the tracks look like at the end but his learning how to do it that counts.

My son wants to touch all my stuff, including my tools. He also wants to open my briefcase, hold my keys, or take the remote. It's driving me nuts!

A curious toddler—what a surprise! Seriously, he's learning about all the stuff that goes along with being a grown-up, especially ones like his idol—Dad. First, be on guard for obvious safety problems—two-year-olds and circular saws obviously don't mix. Put the cool stuff out of the way when you get home—the briefcase goes on a shelf in the coat closet, keys go on a high hook, etc. Then find him some safe "tools" of his own like an old remote or play "work" toys for toddlers. And then play with him when he uses them!

My dad spanked me sometimes. When my son doesn't pay attention, I'm really tempted. I'm surprised at how much my own little boy can tick me off!

It is pretty darned amazing how crazy they can drive you, huh? But hang tough! It's not a lack of respect—toddlers have really, really short attention spans. That's a fact of life, and nothing's going to change that, even swatting his butt. That'll only make him hysterical and make you feel even worse. So don't do it. Just because your dad hit or spanked you—and he likely didn't know any better at the time—doesn't make it a smart way to teach a kid.

Basketball coaches do not hit players for missing a free throw. How would Randy Johnson react if his manager whacked him for allowing a homer? He'd go ballistic. Hitting, slapping, or spanking a kid doesn't work and it only teaches him that *you've exhausted your parenting playbook.* Bench yourself on the sidelines for a bit and take some deep breaths when you feel like you're going to strike him. He'll respect you so much more for your self-control than he would if you hit him.

My son cries when I wash his hair. It really torques me.
Toddlers don't like having their hair washed, period. Think how you'd feel, for instance, if you had a hangover and someone started throwing water over your head. Your job as coach is to figure out a way to get it washed in a way that everybody's a winner. First, just hop in the shower with him. Kids who hate having their hair washed in the bath often don't mind it so much in the shower. And little kids don't really need their hair shampooed more than weekly, so just plain water in the shower can do the trick. Use the smallest amount of baby shampoo possible, if you're washing in the bath. And rinse it with a wet washcloth. It takes a little longer, but it's easier on all the players than dumping water over his head.

I hate seeing my son cry. It makes me snap at him, or I just have to walk away.
Repeat after me: He's just a little kid. Toddlers are little more than babies who can walk, so cut him a break. Little boys cry—period. Every winning coach knows that his job is as much about teaching his athletes to manage their hearts and minds as it is about lifting weights or sprinting times. So don't walk away or yell. Pick him up and help him deal with whatever is bugging him. This stage won't last forever.

My son asks if his penis will be bigger than mine.
Well, duh. Kids are curious about their bodies and about what will happen when they're grown-ups. Just tell him that nobody knows exactly what any kid will look like when he grows up. Sometimes a little boy will even ask you if it'll fall off. Tell him it won't. Tell him you're glad he's a boy and that you wanted a boy.

My son wants to dress himself, and it takes so long it drives me nuts. But he gets so mad if I try to help.

Here's the deal: No quarterback learned to throw the winning pass because his coach rushed in to do it for him in every practice. In other words, chill. Of course it takes him a long time. He's learning a tough new task. Break it down into small bites so he doesn't get overwhelmed, and try to negotiate: "If you put on your socks. I'll do your shoes." Also, give him *plenty* of time to get dressed before going out. He'll get better much faster if you just let him practice.

My wife babies my son's every little whim. It really irritates me.

It can drive the general manager of a baseball team crazy when the pitching coach wants to pull his pitcher off the mound in the sixth inning in a tied game. In other words, experts disagree. What *you* view as babying she might well view as doing what comes natural to a mom. Sometimes there's no right or wrong in parenting, just different styles. You might fear your son will grow up to be a wimp if Mom cuddles him too much, while she thinks he'll end up as some guy named Crusher on the professional wrestling circuit if he doesn't get enough loving. Respect her right to parent the way she wants, and talk to her about what you think. Choose a time when you're not in front of your kid, and avoid talking when everyone feels like they're about to go nuclear. Moms and dads have different ways of parenting, and kids need them *both*. Men don't need to be more like women, and vice versa.

My son hates holding my hand when we cross the street.

Sure he does. He's also not likely crazy about nurses jabbing needles into his arms. But safety comes first. Let him cry, but tell him you're not crossing the street to get to the playground until hands are held. Then offer him a choice: you can carry him or he can walk. Or he can hold your left hand or your right hand. Studies show that kids under the age of ten have a really tough time judging traffic.

CHAPTER 10

Dad of a Girl: Her Protector

You won the lottery. She's adorable! If a safe were falling from the sky, as in cartoons, you would push her aside and take the hit.

But you can't help feeling a little queasy. No matter how much you want to protect her, you can't really follow her around at school. At some point, she's going to have to hold her own in playground politics. If you have anything to do with it, your little girl is going to be smart, successful, and able to defend herself against that mean little seven-year-old punk who looks like he's at least eight.

Fortunately, there are plenty of ways to help your daughter handle the put-downs, the cliques, and other realities of childhood. There are games and activities you can deploy to build daddy-daughter closeness; they're good ways to lay the foundation for a solid relationship and good tools for building self-esteem right from the beginning.

Yes, right now—during the first years of life. This is the perfect time to start preparing your daughter to be a girl who is confident, intelligent, friendly, and who will tell teenage boys, "Sorry, I can't date until I'm twenty-three." (Okay, maybe that last one is beyond your reach.)

If you're thinking, "She's two, I can't possibly teach her anything now," think of it this way: building your little girl's self-esteem is kind of like building a house. It needs a foundation, one that's strong and firm, and that's the first thing that should be constructed. If you don't build a strong foundation to your house, one day you're going to be in your bedroom upstairs, and after screaming and blacking out, you'll wake up in the basement, surrounded by your belongings and covered in brick and plaster. It's kind of the same thing with your daughter. You can't expect to be emotionally unavailable to her for several years, and then just jump in when she's twelve—or four or five—and start giving her pointers about life. She's going to look at you dubiously, as if to say, "And you would be . . . who?"

YOU'RE DRIVING THE CAR, TOO

Some dads might think it's just natural that their girl is going to be closer to Mom, that there's something about a mother's ability to braid pigtails and shop for dresses that means she's the one who really connects with a daughter. But that's a cop-out, and it's really 1950s thinking. What little girl or mom wears dresses that much these days? And it's not just ballet classes these days; your daughter's just as likely to need your help in learning to master soccer or T-ball.

You can't afford to fumble your relationship with your daughter. Loads of research shows that fathers play a powerful role in how a girl views herself as she grows up—and how she handles romantic relationships. Think about it. If you're not very communicative with your little girl, you're sending her a message that she's not worth getting to know, and you may well be inspiring her to pick out boyfriends and husbands who won't give her the time of day, either. Worse, you might even unknowingly be sending her on the path to being in an abusive relationship someday, because while that jerk beats her up, at least he's paying attention to her.

HIGH STAKES

Scary, isn't it? You're probably starting to think that interacting with your little girl is kind of like planning to light a match during a gas leak. One false move, and *kablooey!* You've screwed up your kid for life. It's not that bad, of course, though if you dwell on it long enough, it can feel that way.

And if that isn't alarming enough, research also shows that your relationship with your daughter can help determine her success in school, sports, whether she'll go to college, and whether she'll start smoking or using drugs.

It all starts now. That little adorable toddler with jam on her face, the one who would rather watch Elmo than Tiger Woods—she is looking for your guidance.

So you can either reluctantly wade into your parenting duties or jump in like an enthusiastic coach—and embrace the idea that she's going to be looking to you, in large part, to learn how to make her way independently through life.

You can start by letting her learn how to make good decisions and choices, rather than always making them for her. Obviously, you have to make some of the choices. Riding in her car seat isn't open to debate. But you can let her make the choice between wearing shorts or a skirt. You can let her decide what type of sandwich she'll have for lunch. If she wants to wear her winter coat in June, let her. She'll quickly figure out it's too hot without you telling her.

ENCOURAGE HER

If you're thinking, "Hey, you're preaching to the choir—I love my daughter. I'd take a bullet for her. I'd go on *Fear Factor* and eat glass, if I had to," then, great. But keep in mind that some well-meaning, loving dads tend to be overly protective with their precious cargo. Yes, she's a little girl, but she isn't made of glass. It's important to occasionally risk a skinned knee and not immediately rush in to help or stop her from doing something that could teach her something valuable. If she wants to try climbing a ladder at the playground, don't tell her she's too little—unless it's painfully obvious that she is, of course.

Instead, if you can, try to figure out a way for her to do it safely, like standing behind her to catch her if she slips. That way she'll know you're confident in her ability to learn new things, but you are there to back her up if she needs it. It's like when your uncle taught you to fish. You never would have learned how to do it if he'd always baited the hook, cast the line, and cleaned the catch, right? He let you drop his prize worms into the water and he hardly said a word, even when your hook stabbed him in his thigh and he screamed, and he jumped to his feet and he rocked the boat, and he pitched forward into the lake. Well, the point is, thanks to your uncle not interfering, you learned to fish.

Another difficult area for any dad to deal with is fights with playmates. If the fight is over a toy, see if they can work things out before you jump in to help her out. With younger toddlers, by all means cut in if you think another child could really hurt yours; say, if that kid is about to conk her on the head with a wooden block, or if that boy has shoved her off playground equipment. If she gets slugged by another kid, you're going to hate this advice—but take a quick mental note on how hard she was hit, because no matter what just happened, obviously your instinct is to take this kid down, beat him into a pulp, and then go after his family.

But because we're assuming this little playground punk is maybe three or four years old, that would really be wrong.

Instead:

1. If your daughter has just been hit lightly and there are no tears, just watch carefully and see if she can work things out for herself.
2. If there are tears, calm your daughter down and remove her from the holy terror. Chances are, his mom or dad is coming to the scene to help out. This is great, because if it's the dad then you can tackle him to the ground, make like Clint Eastwood, and—no, no, it was just a fleeting thought. Instead, be civil and assume that his parents are just as mortified as you, because they probably are.
3. Once you're alone with your daughter, you can talk about what to do next time if the same thing happens (and you

know it will). Even though you like the Clint Eastwood idea, counsel her to walk away if another kid hits her.

And don't be too hard on the other kid or his parents—your little angel may well be the one swinging a mean left hook the next time you're at the park!

NO, NO, NO . . . NO . . .

You heard it as a child from your parents. You heard it when you propositioned Sheila McGillicuddy in the backseat of your car. You hear it from your wife. You hear it from your boss. And, now, you're hearing it from your little girl.

It can be a little jolting. Your little sweetie, who sometimes seems to worship the ground you walk on, is staring at you and saying "No."

It may be hard to swallow, but you have to recognize that your daughter isn't being obstinate, she's practicing the concept of control—and sometimes, you should give in. If she doesn't want to wear her shoes in the backyard, and you want her to because it's cool outside, this might be the time to just nod and agree. Your daughter should get a say in what she's doing, occasionally.

Look at it this way. Someday your daughter's going to be Sheila McGillicuddy, and when she's tangling with a teenage octopus, what do you hope she's confident enough to say?

BE POSITIVE ABOUT HER LOOKS

It's important not to tease your little girl about what she looks like, or what she weighs, even at this young age. Girls whose fathers negatively comment on their appearance can develop low self-esteem and even eating disorders. And nobody wants their little girl to grow up and become anorexic.

The opposite is true, too. Constantly commenting on her beauty to the exclusion of anything else can lead her to believe that you think it's the most important thing about her—more than her intelligence, her goofy humor, and how well she's learning to brush her teeth.

So take your enthusiasm for her appearance down a few notches, and when you're doling out the compliments for everything else, don't be stingy. Maybe the block building she's putting together would make Frank Lloyd Wright spin in his grave, but just show her that you're glad she's learning: "I like your cool block tower."

"Close to the Coach"

One to three years

Whisper a secret only Dad and daughter know about. Dad will *always* be numero uno!

• Hold your daughter close.
• Tell her you are happy to see her and you missed her.
• Say, "I'm so glad you're my girl!"
• Say, "I'm proud to be your dad!"

Game tip: *Connect daily with a hug and a whispered word.*

"Daddy Rocks"

One to three years

Flash back to your high school prom and take your little girl for a spin around the dance floor. You are introducing her to rhythm and helping her coordination—something she'll need if she takes ballet or plays sports.

- Put on a favorite CD. Try a variety, from salsa to classical.
- Pick your daughter up and dance around the room. Add twirls and dips for a thrill.
- Serenade your little girl.
- Play a dancing form of follow-the-leader. Follow your daughter's lead, and then have her copy your moves.

Game tip: *Tambourines and maracas are great musical additions.*

"Bathing Baby with Dad"

One to three years

Get down with Dad for the cleanup! Practice taking turns and making friends for the kindergarten playground.

- Cleanup and bath time are fun with Dad.
- Offer your daughter choices about which doll takes a bath.
- Use different voices and pretend dolls are talking to each other.

Game tip: *Bath time or at the pool is another good time to give dolls a bath.*

"Feeding the Mascot"

One to three years

Imaginary play helps kids learn the differences between fantasy and reality.

- Offer your daughter a choice of two stuffed animals.
- Use a kitty voice saying, "Meow, I'm hungry."
- Feed the animals.
- Take the animals for a pretend walk or ride.
- Put the animals down to sleep together for a nap.

Game tip: *Give one of the animals your child's name, and another of the animals your name.*

"Most Valuable Player"

Eighteen months to three years

Every little girl wants some solo time with Daddy, and here's a way to build spatial concepts and self-confidence.

• Throw a blanket over your head, with part of your head visible, and ask, "Where's Daddy?"
• After your child has uncovered your partially hidden head a couple of times, cover yourself entirely and say, "Come find me!" Cheer and say, "You did it! You found me!" and give her a kiss.

Game tip: *A special hideaway such as a small tent or large cardboard box or table with a sheet makes for a great fort. Climb on in, and share a book, a game, or tell stories.*

"Tackling the Coach"

Eighteen months to three years

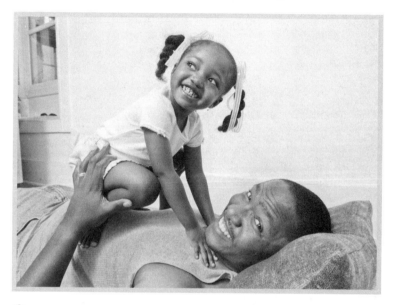

Connect with your kid while you work on your abs six-pack. If your child is timid, she'll gain confidence. If your child is ready for the NBA, she'll understand how it feels when others get pushed. It is important in this activity to keep things friendly, so your child understands the difference between pushing and pushing people around. This is a handy skill to have on hand when defending against bullies.

- Lie on the floor or sofa with a pillow under your head.
- Put your child on your chest in a sitting position, facing you.
- Sit halfway up and let your child push you down.

Game tip: *Soft surfaces are the best place to play this game.*

241

"Tailgate Tea Party"

One to three years

Your little girl will gain an appreciation for conversation and excellent manners when she has a tea party with one of her favorite guests—her dad. It will also give her a chance to practice sharing and social skills.

- Break out a tea set and serve up some yummies—cookies, crackers, or tiny sandwiches.
- Invite a few guests—perhaps a doll or two, or some favorite stuffed animals.
- Practice serving each other, using your best *please*s and *thank-you*s.

Game tip: *Toy stores sell plastic fruits and vegetables made with Velcro, which kids are able to "cut" apart with a plastic knife.*

"The Hair Challenge"

One to three years

*G*etting out of the house in the morning with a toddler is a big job. It's time to have your little girl do her part. Develop her sense of independence, her attention span, and her listening skills. She'll start strengthening her arms, too—something every budding softball star needs.

• Put your girl in front of a mirror.
• Give her a small child-sized hairbrush.
• Ask, "Where's your hair?"
• Begin brushing her hair, starting at the ends to the scalp, to get rid of·tangles.
• Put the brush in her hand, and guide it through her hair.
• Let her do it herself if she wants to and then do a quick run-through to finish the job.

Game tip: *A soft brush works better than a comb.*

TIPS FOR WINNING

Help her become independent by helping her learn how to dress herself and feed herself.

Let her help you around the house on chores or jobs she can handle, like putting the napkins on the dinner table or the kibbles in the dog's dish.

Teach her how to meet new people. Show her how to shake hands, and how to make eye contact.

It's important to let your girl know you value her for more than her looks. Don't fake your praise, but look for opportunities to let her know how proud you are that she's learning her colors or trying to use a fork.

Don't make fun of or tease a girl about her physical appearance. You might think it's cute to poke her "baby fat" or call her your little pudgy bear, but it can slam her harder than being taken down by an NFL lineman.

Accept the fact that sometimes your daughter will want to be Daddy's little girl, and not want to share you, even with Mom. Of course, without warning, sometimes she'll just want Mom. It's better not to even try to figure it out.

SAFETY ZONE

When you're out alone with your girl and your toddler is getting to the potty-training stage, it's time for your hyper-vigilant gene to kick in. You must never, *never* leave your little girl alone, even if you need to use the restroom for just an instant. Try to find a unisex family restroom, and if you can't, consider going into that men's room with your daughter. She's unlikely to see anything you don't want her to see, with everybody's front being to the wall and her not knowing to look over there, anyway. And the guys in there aren't likely to care; your daughter won't be the first toddler they've ever seen in the restroom. Just take her into the stall with you, lock the door, sit down, and do your business if you have to. Sure, it might sound distasteful, but as long as you're discreet and able to cover up what you need to cover up, chances are she's going to be more mesmerized by the drain on the floor, or the tiles on the floor, than being preoccupied with what you're doing.

Never, ever ask a stranger to watch your child while you go out of sight, no matter how safe he looks. In this day and age, even a mother-and-daughter combo might not be so great. If you're thinking that "stranger danger" isn't all that serious, the papers were full of stories several years ago about a man in Seattle who got the name "Santa Claus" for how much he looked like that jolly old elf. What made him newsworthy? He was a child molester.

Another important safety tip: male relatives, your sister's boyfriend, and teenage boys really aren't swell picks for babysitters. Obviously, some can be as terrific as any woman.

But keep in mind that some men can be unpredictable when it comes to kids, even predatory, and it can be really tough to tell before problems occur. Many molesters are very charming or disarming—it's how they're able to victimize children for years before being caught. It's not a risk you want to assume with your child, female or male.

Emotional safety: When you and your partner fight, avoid yelling as much as possible. It's scary for your daughter and counterproductive for you. It's also upsetting for her if you sulk or withdraw during family disputes.

SPECIAL PLAYS

One way to build a bond with your daughter is to develop routines just for the two of you. It can be something as simple as a regular date at the park to learn how to kick a soccer ball or play catch. Make it a regular occurrence, not something you do only when you remember it, if and when you have time. If you have a demanding work schedule, try actually writing it on your calendar so it doesn't slip by.

Find something you can do every day together, like a special breakfast or a night-night story session. She'll love it. And look at it this way: when you're old and gray, and your little daughter is shopping around for your retirement home, maybe she'll remember those moments and make sure you get a room with a view.

Along those lines, think about creating a dad-and-daughter night out, something that only the two of you share. Mom would enjoy the break, and you'll love the closeness the two of you will feel as a result. Find a local pizza restaurant to frequent, or an ice cream store. It's not how much money you spend, it's the time you spend together. You can wash the car together, or bring in the mail or the newspapers. Maybe she could help put fallen leaves in a basket. And there's an added bonus to this: small, regular chores fill toddlers with pride and a sense of accomplishment, something all children need.

Do you want to get a few extra minutes reading the sports pages? Sit together with your daughter and scan the paper. Point out stories about female athletes. Girls who play sports have a healthy body image. Remind your wife about that the next time the channel is turned to ESPN.

Find books or make up stories about girls who overcome obstacles or challenges, or who invent things.

Choose videos and make up stories about girls who fix things or solve problems. Puppets can also be used to tell stories about smart or brave girls. Take stories like "Little Red Riding Hood" or "Sleeping Beauty" and make up new endings. Substitute your daughter's name for the heroine.

Encourage your little girl to pretend she's a doctor. Have her fix your boo-boos or heal her stuffed animals. A kid's medical kit, even a box of Band-Aids, will ramp up the fun.

When she has the coordination, teach her to use a toy screwdriver and hammer with plastic nuts and bolts, using a tool bench made for kids.

CALL FOR THE REFEREE

Your wife often sends your daughter to her room during a dispute, but you think she's too hard on her. You don't know what to do, and your superhero sense is telling you that to take your daughter's side could result in your sleeping in the garage again. They often fight about clothes, what your daughter wants to wear. Well, your wife needs to know that sending a toddler to her room is pretty ineffective at that age. Her attention span is so short that she's likely to end up more confused or upset than anything else. Tell your wife your views on the problem, and feel free to show her this paragraph if you need backup. Ask her if there aren't some better ways to handle the issue. Suggest just giving your little girl a limited number of acceptable clothing choices, and putting others, like swimsuits or snow pants, out of sight. Make up a list of behaviors that tick you and Mom off, and brainstorm or reach agreement on what the consequences should be. And then, because your wife is frustrated that you never discipline your daughter but are always happy to give Mom advice, make sure that before you have this conversation, there are warm blankets and a pillow in the garage.

Every night when you want to give your daughter her bath or read her a book, she insists she only wants Mom. It really bums you out. Understandable, but know that you're not the first dad in the history of the world to make that complaint. Little kids are very connected to the person who's with them the most during their earliest years, the person who gave them the most physical care. In many cases, that means Mom. The good news is that as kids grow older and out of toddlerhood, that changes. The day may come when your girl gives Mom the cold shoulder in favor of you (try not to gloat). But for now, try sharing the bathroom chores. Sit in there with Mom while your girl bathes. Hand your daughter the pajamas when you're both getting your toddler ready for bed. If Mom's the one who reads to her, sit in and turn the pages for her. And don't give up. Chances are your daughter's testing you, waiting to see, and hoping that you're really sincere about being involved.

Your wife always wants you to take your little precious girl to the doctor for her shots, and you don't want to, because you don't want to be known as the monster who takes your daughter to the bad man with the needle. "Besides," you tell your wife, "this is really your department. You always call the shots around here. Hahaha-hahah, heheheheh . . . heehee . . . Sorry, I'll go get my car keys . . ." And why shouldn't you take the little darling to the doctor? Nothing in the parenting playbook says one parent or the other has to do it, and while you may be taking your daughter to her needle doom, you'll also get to be the one who comforts her when the shot is over. That said, the best idea is for both parents to go, so your little girl understands how important you both think it is. Also, there's no reason to tell her in advance she's going to have shots. That will just work her up for no reason. You can explain it to her while the vaccines are being prepared. Then take her out for a treat, like a milk shake or a trip to the park, for being such a brave girl. It's also handy to have a few stickers or other small surprises ready to give her immediately after the shot.

ADVICE FROM THE COACH

When I get back from a business trip, my daughter wants me to drop everything and spend time with her. But I feel like I have so much to catch up on!

Of course you do—and that includes catching up with your daughter. Not that I don't sympathize. The sheer amount of juggling that career and fathering takes, on top of chores like mowing lawns, cleaning, and taking the dog to the vet, can make any man feel like he's running a marathon every day. But the deal is, your daughter wants desperately to reconnect with you. To her, even a day or two away from Daddy feels like forever. So take some time and focus just on her. Take her to the park, read some books together, or just sit her in your lap and tell her about your trip. Don't try to do anything else during this time or cut it short. This will help her feel like she's still important to Dad, and that he missed her, too. You can squeeze in everything else while she's in bed, or when she inevitably wants to watch some cartoon. Nobody says on his deathbed, "I remember that Saturday afternoon when I could have gone to the park, but I'm so glad I cleaned out those storm gutters instead. Honey—*gasp, ack*—before I go, pass me that scrapbook of the gutters . . ."

I'm finding it hard to know what little girls like to do. I don't want to play with dolls.

So don't. Moms and dads play in different ways, and with different toys, and both are equally cool in helping girls grow up. If you want to play with blocks, do it. She'll learn all kinds of lessons about building, geometry, and patience. If you like to always be moving, by all means, be a bucking bronco—a friendly bucking bronco—and give your girl a ride around the den. Build her a playhouse, and help her sort nuts and bolts in your shop. Don't think there's only one way to play with a girl. She'll be the better—and smarter—for learning new ways to play.

When we go hiking, I want my daughter to walk. She wants to be held, but I don't want her to wimp out.
Good for you. Maybe you should let her carry your backpack while you're at it. And if you're nodding with approval, let me say this slowly: I-waaaaaas-beeeeing-sarcaaaaastic. Little toddlers don't wimp out. What you want is something a little kid can't give you. You can't expect a two-year-old to walk more than a block or two at a time. As she gets older, you can expect a little more. Think very short walks, not hiking, and both of you will have a better time.

My daughter is very strong-willed. I don't want to break her spirit, but I don't want to give in all the time. I almost always do, though, because I don't like to see her sad.
When you give in all the time, you teach her a very important lesson, but maybe one she shouldn't be learning: that she can get her own way, despite what Dad wants. Is that something you want her to take into her teenage years, when she starts driving and dating? Didn't think so. Discipline is not about breaking anyone's spirit. It's about teaching your daughter how to manage herself and her emotions, to obey important safety rules, and to learn how to get along with

others. Screw this up, and I guarantee nobody's going to want to play with a rude, self-centered kid, in school or on the soccer team. Yes, she might be sad in the short term when she doesn't get her way on everything, but she's also going to be scared if she always does get her way. She relies on you to be one of her head coaches, and when you don't do it, that means nobody's in control—and that's scary. So stick to your guns, and gently but firmly enforce the house rules.

I don't know what to do when my daughter takes another kid's toy. She sometimes is a bully.

Toddlers have zero sense of sharing. It is something you and Mom will work on for the next few years. When you see this happen, take the toy away and tell her matter-of-factly, "We don't take other people's things." Repeat several hundred times until she gets the point.

My daughter is really shy. She won't let us leave her with her grandmother, a babysitter, or a play group. She just glues herself to my side.

Shyness is one of those things you're born with. But you can help her slowly get more comfortable with the bigger world; it just takes a lot more time than it does with more outgoing toddlers. Expose her to new experiences slowly and consistently. Don't give up on Grandma. Take her there, and bring a new toy. While she's playing by herself with you and Grandma nearby, go into another room, but stay where she can see you. Repeat on several different occasions. Then, one of the times, leave—she'll likely cry—but come back after ten minutes. Gradually lengthen the time you stay away. She'll learn eventually that you're not deserting her, and she'll gain some pride in her growing independence. Just don't expect her to turn into the life of the party. She is who she is.

My daughter cries when her mother goes out. I don't know what to do.
This is incredibly common, and it doesn't reflect how much she loves you. Often Mom was the center of the world during babyhood, because she probably did most of the child care. Help your daughter by doing practice runs of short periods, gradually lengthening the time Mom stays away. This anxiety will gradually go away as your toddler gets older, but it takes time. It can help to have a special treat or video she gets only when Mom is gone. Or try a game that only Daddy does—like flying her around like an airplane.

My daughter wants to comb my hair, and she wants me to play house and have me be the mom or the baby.
Kids this little just don't understand rigid gender roles. If you're uncomfortable with playing house or beauty parlor, just steer her into another activity, like playing with stuffed animals or making music. Ask her if you can be a puppy instead of a mommy. She's got plenty of time to figure out families.

My daughter says she wants to be a boy and wants a penis. You can only imagine what starts going through my head. What should I say to her?
Believe it or not, this is not uncommon among little kids, who always seem to want what they don't have and are deeply curi-

ous about the differences between boys and girls. Assure her she has a perfectly nice body, you're glad she is a girl, and she isn't lacking for anything. Keep it light. Toddlers are too young to take in complicated explanations about anatomy and will just blank out if you try.

Appendix

Toddler Behavior:
What to Expect and
How to Deal with It

What sorts of behavior are normal for your toddler, and how should you respond? Here's a sampling of the drive-you-crazy behavior you're likely to encounter, and some strategies you can use.

SPEECH	AGE RANGE	STRATEGIES
Whining	1–3 years	Say, "I cannot understand you when you use that voice. Tell me again in a different voice."
Grunts and yells loudly when unhappy	1–2½ years	Say to your child, "You are mad." The parent demonstrates a "mad face" and says, "Speak quietly. Show me your mad face. Use your words to say *mad* quietly."
Screams when having a haircut	1–2 years	Play barber at home. Take your child with you to watch when you get a haircut. Let him sit in

SPEECH	AGE RANGE	STRATEGIES
		your lap when getting a haircut. Have a reward at the end of your child's haircut.
Ignores request to come (refuses to listen)	1–2 years	Say, "Come here." Make eye contact and place your hand on the child's shoulder. Say, "You can come by yourself, or I will help you come. I think you can come all by yourself."
Screams "No!" when requested to stop certain behaviors	1–3 years	Say, "You need to stop. I will count to three. One, two, three. Stop now." Emphasize the word *now*. Repeat the request and tell the child there will be a consequence if he doesn't stop. For example, "I will take away your toy if you don't stop banging it on the table."
Stutters	1–3 years	Ignore, be patient, and wait for your child to finish speaking. Do not finish sentences for the child; do not let others comment on stuttering.
Doesn't talk but gestures—lifts arms to be picked up	1–2 years	Say to your child, "You want up." Repeat, "Up, up, up." Ask your child to say the word *up*.
Doesn't seem to understand requests or ignores request	1–2 years	Get your child's attention, including eye contact. Demonstrate your request through actions or gesture. For example, if your child won't stop banging his toy, put your hand on his to stop the banging and say, "Stop banging."

Points to what is wanted—for example, goes to the refrigerator	1–2 years	Pointing is a good form of communication for a toddler age 1 to 2 years. Encourage children over 2 to "use your words." Model the request, "Want a drink, please."

BEHAVIOR	AGE RANGE	STRATEGIES
Refuses to brush teeth, wash hands, get dressed	1–3 years	Make statements to your child rather than asking questions. For example, say, "It's time to brush your teeth," rather than, "Do you want to brush your teeth?" If she persists in saying "No," ignore it and proceed with completing the task.
Defies parent just to see what will happen	2–3 years	Give one warning and then follow through with a consequence: for example, losing a privilege such as watching a video or TV for the day.
Throws toys	1–2 years	Say, "Toys are for playing." Provide warning/direction: "Toys stay on the floor, otherwise the toys will go up and away."
Pushing, kicking, or hitting other children or adults	1–3 years	Say, "Stop." Get between your child and the other child. Take a short time-out of one to three minutes nearby. Say "Sorry" to the victim.
Taking toys or food from other children	1–3 years	Everything is "mine" to a toddler. Provide adult supervision and direction to prevent your child from taking other children's toys or food.

BEHAVIOR	AGE RANGE	STRATEGIES
Bites others in the play group	1–2 years	Get face-to-face with your child and say, "No biting. Biting hurts." Give the child a one- to two-minute time-out nearby and a soft rubber teether to chew regularly.
Won't share toys	1–3 years	Kids this age don't share. Have lots of duplicate toys. Put special one-of-a-kind toys away.
Cries when parents leave for the evening/ fearful of strangers	1–3 years	Practice peekaboo, hide-and-seek, going into the other room and coming back. Have new sitters come and stay awhile with you and your child before you leave. Give your child some object that belongs to you to hold until you return.
Takes things that belong to others— everything's "mine"	1–3 years	What's yours is mine and what's mine is mine! Toddlers have no concept of ownership. Put keys, purses, briefcases, phones, and remote controls out of reach. Give him some adult look-alike equivalents for play.

MAKING MESSES	AGE RANGE	STRATEGIES
Dumps out the wastebasket/ garbage can	1–2 years	Put garbage and wastebaskets out of reach.
Tears out the pages in his book; chews on books	1–2 years	Have cardboard books for toddlers. If she's teething, offer substitutes for chewing.

Gets into your purse or briefcase and strews items on the floor	1–2 years	Put the purse and briefcase out of reach. Be sure they are closed; do not keep medications or dangerous items stored inside. Have a play purse or briefcase for your child to play with.
Takes clothes out of drawers	1–3 years	State, "Clothes stay in drawers." Have the toddler help replace all items. Provide your child with a box of two to three clothing items that can be dress-up clothes.
Trashes his room or play area	1–3 years	Cut down on the number of toys. Show your toddler that when he makes a mess, he has to help clean it up. Work with him to put the toys away.
Throws stuff (including expensive stuff, like your cell phone)	1–2 years	Keep your cell phone out of reach. Tell your toddler, "Anything that's thrown goes away for the day." Put those toys up on a high shelf.
Takes things apart; for instance, pulling the knobs off your electronic equipment	1–3 years	Restrict access to electronic equipment by putting it on a high shelf.
Pushes buttons on the VCR or TV, or messes with your computer	1–3 years	Cover the computer with a drop cloth or secure it behind doors when not in use. Restrict access to VCRs as much as possible using a VCR toddler lockout device. Buy push-button toys or give your child an old keyboard or telephone.

MAKING MESSES	AGE RANGE	STRATEGIES
Squeezes toothpaste out of tube, or unrolls toilet paper	1–3 years	Keep those items secured and/or out of reach of the child.
Gets into forbidden drawers, closets, or shelves	1–3 years	*Off limits* is a concept foreign to toddlers. Install child-safe locks to restrict access to any drawer or shelf that the child should not touch.
Scribbles on walls or sofa	1–3 years	Be sure all markers, crayons, and writing utensils are secure and only available with close one-to-one adult supervision. If the child attempts to leave the art area, immediately require her to put the markers on the table and say, "The markers, paints, or crayons need to stay on the table."

FRUSTRATING BEHAVIOR	AGE RANGE	STRATEGIES
Expresses anger physically—pushes or hits	1–2 years	Time out, held in a chair if necessary. One to two minutes.
Cries when the parents are out of sight; for example, a parent is in the bathroom and the child wants to come in	1–3 years	Talk to your child through the door: "I will be there in a moment." Help the child learn that you return when you're gone.
Lies down on the floor in protest	1–3 years	Reflect the child's feelings to her: "You are mad." Offer an alternative: "Come sit by me. I will give you a hug." Tell her, "I know you will pull yourself together."

Is frustrated when he wants something and you don't know what it is	1–3 years	Ask the child to show you, using gestures. Ask your child questions for clarification that can be answered with "yes" or "no."
Ignores your request/ continues behavior when asked to stop	1–3 years	Get your child's visual attention. Make your request of the desired behavior using gestures. Help the child comply as necessary. Provide praise, to reinforce following parental requests.
Pulls or hangs on a parent/won't walk alone	1–3 years	Carry the child or put him in a stroller.
Defies you— says "No!" when you tell him to do something	1–3 years	Say, "You don't want to." Get down to your child's eye level, and slowly and clearly repeat the request. "It's time to _____. You can do it yourself or I will help you. I think you can do what I said by yourself, and I will be very proud of you."
SAFETY	**AGE RANGE**	**STRATEGIES**
Doesn't want to be confined; has trouble sitting in a shopping cart or stroller while shopping; wants to get out and walk, or whines	1–2 years	Reflect the child's feelings. One hour is the maximum a child can be expected to sit in a shopping cart or stroller while shopping. Comment on your surroundings; have a toy for the child to hold to distract him. Carry on a conversation about your activity: "Now we're going to get milk. What does a cow say?"

SAFETY	AGE RANGE	STRATEGIES
Cries when placed in the car seat	1–2 years	Say, "I know sometimes you don't want to sit in your car seat." Have special car-only toys for distraction; tell stories; comment on or ask questions about the trip while traveling.
Won't sit longer than three minutes without wanting to move	1–3 years	Accept that toddlers have a great need for physical activity; review whether it is necessary that the child remain still; offer distractions such as a small toy or a book.
Undoes car seat harness	1–3 years	Check the fittings to be sure they are in good working order. Consider replacing the car seat—perhaps your toddler is ready to move up to the next size? If the child undoes the harness while driving, stop as soon as possible, refasten it, and explain, "We cannot drive if your car seat is not fastened."
Runs away after being taken out of the car seat/stroller: acts like it's a game in a store or parking lot	2–3 years	Do not give your child the opportunity to run. Hold her hand or carry her from the car seat directly into the stroller.
Doesn't want to get back in the car after a break during a car trip	1–3 years	Travel during nap time or in the evening. Distract her by keeping small books and toys in the car. Buy a DVD or CD player and play DVDs or CDs on lengthy car trips.

Pulls a "Tarzan"— climbing the drapes, the furniture, etc., even after you've told him not to	1–3 years	Purchase a small slide or an inflatable punching bag. Provide indoor outlets for physical activity. For example, jump on pillows placed on the floor. If possible, go outside for a walk to the park.
At the playground, climbs to the top of the bars and then lets go, doesn't understand danger	1–3 years	Toddlers do *not* understand danger. Provide a safety net by being there one to two feet behind them.
Sticks pencils, beans, paper, etc., up the nose or in ears	1–3 years	Restrict access to anything sharp, pointed, or small that can be used in such a fashion.
Tries to step off the top of a flight of stairs	1–2 years	Teach your toddler the safe way to go up and down stairs—backward—and provide close supervision.
Doesn't want to sit in the stroller for walks	1–3 years	Purchase a toy bar, made especially for strollers, with toys attached that move and make noise.

SELF-CARE	AGE RANGE	STRATEGIES
Protests having her teeth brushed	1–3 years	Practice brushing Dad's teeth. Play with the toothbrush in the tub.
Resists having her hair brushed	1–3 years	Brush the child's hair from the ends first. Let your child comb Dad's hair. Play barber or beauty shop.

SELF-CARE	AGE RANGE	STRATEGIES
Pees after standing up to take a bath; pees/poops on the floor	2–3 years	Remember, he's just learning to control what has been automatic before. Help by directing him immediately onto the potty after clothes are removed.
Likes to put toys in the toilet, tries to play in the toilet	1–3 years	Put a safety latch on the toilet seat
Repeatedly flushes the toilet	1–3 years	Put a childproof doorknob cover on the bathroom door. Let him flush the toilet when he uses it. Keep the bathroom door closed.
Unrolls toilet paper	1–3 years	Put the paper out of reach. This is one temptation that is very difficult to resist!
Is reluctant to sit on the potty	1–3 years	Start him by sitting on the potty with his clothes on. Put a teddy bear or doll on the potty. Gradually move him to sitting on the potty with his pants down for only a short time. Celebrate first successes with great fanfare!
Takes contents of the diaper out and smears it on the walls or bedding	1–3 years	Toddlers are naturally curious, and this action is just an extension of that curiosity. With younger toddlers, use clothing that restrains their access to the diaper: overalls with snaps, full-length sleepers with zippers. Change your child promptly. It is best not to leave the child alone in the crib with a dirty diaper.

GETTING DRESSED	AGE RANGE	STRATEGIES
Resists being changed; doesn't want to lie down to be changed	1–2 years	Offer an incentive to your child: "Diaper first, and then we'll wrestle." Let her help select her clothing or choose from several diapers with different patterns. Say, "Do you want the diaper with dinosaurs or cars?" Sing along; make it a game. Give your toddler something to hold that she only gets on the changing table. Consider moving to changing and dressing on the floor.
Refuses to get dressed or struggles	1–3 years	Get dressed watching TV or videos. Practice rhymes and songs while dressing; play peekaboo; let your child help select clothing; work fast.
Takes shoes/socks off after being dressed	1–3 years	This one is inevitable. It's a step to learning how to get dressed and undressed by himself. If the child repeatedly removes his shoes and socks, have him walk a short distance outside without shoes and socks.
Removes hat and throws it down	1–3 years	Most toddlers hate hats. Purchase hats with elastic or Velcro fasteners that the child cannot remove.

GETTING DRESSED	AGE RANGE	STRATEGIES
Refuses to put on his coat	1–3 years	Use natural consequences. Go outside without a coat and let him get cold, and then put the coat on. Say, "You get cold when you go outside without a coat on."

EATING BEHAVIOR	AGE RANGE	STRATEGIES
Won't eat vegetables	1–3 years	Offer a small amount without comment; mix with other food; give food a personalized name: "Here's the Hannah broccoli tree." Provide a small cup with ranch dip or blue cheese dip for vegetables.
Only wants to eat one or two foods	1–3 years	This is normal. Continue to offer a variety, as well as the one or two he wants to eat. Mix favorite foods with other new foods—for example, macaroni and cheese and peas, noodles and shredded carrots.
Only eats a few bites, and wants to be done and get down	1–3 years	This is completely normal. Toddlers eat less than you think they need.
Won't be fed by parents—wants to feed herself and makes a mess	1–3 years	It's time to let her start, mess or no mess. Start with the least messy options, like small squares of bread or fruit, and small pieces of diced chicken. Help your child learn to use the spoon.

Throws food from the high-chair tray or turns the plate, cup, or bowl of food upside down or throws them down	1–3 years	It's time to end the meal; remove the food and utensils.
Makes a huge mess in restaurants—food on the floor, table, and chair	1–3 years	That is how it is, eating with a toddler in a restaurant. Give him only a small amount of food at a time. Bring a few small (and quiet) toys or a coloring book and crayons.

SLEEP	AGE RANGE	STRATEGIES
Doesn't want to go to bed; cries when put into bed	1–3 years	After completing the hug, story, and bedtime routine, say, "It's time to go to sleep now." Play soft music or activate crib toys.
Wakes in the night and cries	1–3 years	Go in and comfort her; try to calm her without picking her up. Rub or pat the child's back and say, "Go back to sleep." Keep lights dim or use a night-light.
Wakes in the night and wants to nurse or have a bottle	1–3 years	Comfort him and say, "You're okay, go back to sleep." Give the child a pacifier. Activate the crib toy.
Wants to sleep in the parents' bed	1–3 years	Redirect and replace her in her own bed. Provide a colored flashlight. Place large photos of the parents around

SLEEP	AGE RANGE	STRATEGIES
		the crib or bed. Give her a familiar stuffed toy or blanket. Pat her back.
Wakes up because the pacifier has fallen out of his mouth	1–3 years	Leave a couple of extra pacifiers in the crib—*never* with strings attached; those can strangle a child.

Acknowledgments

Above all, thank you to my daughter, Kate, who had to spend a lot of Saturdays helping with the photo shoots, and for putting up with my having to write much of this book during the evenings. I am very lucky I get to be your mom. You are a great kid! Thanks, certainly, to Jan Klits and Josh Caldwell for the emergency computer first aid and advice. To Gloria Coronado and Pam Bissell, who are always willing to listen and offer excellent insight and support. My deepest appreciation and everlasting gratitude to Erika Holmes, a.k.a. Superwoman, who is my trusty assistant and who was willing to do whatever was needed to get this book done from beginning to end, including viewing endless photos. I'm so glad we work together. You are terrific!

To all the contributors, especially Geoff Williams, for his excellent writing and humor. To Alison Blake, Rachel Trindle, Jessica Lane, Leigh Perks, Marge Manwaring, and Elaine Porterfield; each and every one of you added to the book in your own way.

Dan DeLong, Julie Koo, and Jane Lee—thank you for all the wonderful photographs and for your patience in photographing mobile toddlers.

To George Lucas, my first editor at Simon and Schuster,

who believed in this project at the beginning, for your continuing kindness and support. Many thanks also to Micki Nuding, who "adopted" the Rookie Dad series; thanks for your openness, excellent organization, and taking the book to the finish line.

To my agents, Arnold and Elise Goodman, I admire and respect you. Thank you for believing in me and for finding a home for this book.

To all the folks at Microsoft: Grace Wang, who posted the first Microsoft parenting seminars for me, and Stella Yang, who kept it going for its first year. Especially to Xue-Ling Han, who has taken the time to coordinate the parenting seminars at Microsoft for me for the past three years. I am so grateful for your help.

And finally, I offer my thanks to all the dads and moms at Microsoft who have taken time from their busy work schedules to attend parenting seminars, ask questions, share their experiences, and come to photo shoots.

Index